DAISY WASHBURN OSBORN

THE
WOMAN
BELIEVER

BOOKS BY DAISY AND T.L. OSBORN

BIG LOVE PLAN
FIVE CHOICES FOR WOMEN WHO WIN
THE GOOD LIFE
GOSPEL ACCORDING TO T.L. AND DAISY
HEALING THE SICK -- A LIVING CLASSIC
HOW TO BE BORN AGAIN
LIFE'S GREATEST ACHIEVEMENT
100 DIVINE HEALING FACTS
OPT FOR OPPORTUNITY
OUTSIDE THE SANCTUARY
POWER OF POSITIVE DESIRE
RECEIVE MIRACLE HEALING
RHAPSODY OF REALITIES
SEEDS TO SUCCEED
SOULWINNING -- OUT WHERE THE PEOPLE ARE
THE BEST OF LIFE
THE WOMAN BELIEVER
THERE'S PLENTY FOR YOU
TWO-WAY TOUCH
WOMAN BE FREE!
WOMEN ON BEAM -- WINNING WITH ESTEEM
WOMAN WITHOUT LIMITS
YOU ARE GOD'S BEST

For these and other titles, write to:

OSFO PUBLISHERS
Box 10, Tulsa, OK 74102

Publisher

OSFO International

USA WORLD HQ: BOX 10, TULSA, OK 74102

AUSTRALIA: BOX 54, GPO, SYDNEY, NSW 2001

CANADA: BOX 281, ADELAIDE ST POST STA, TORONTO, M5C 2J4

ENGLAND: BOX 148 BIRMINGHAM B3 3EQ

NEW ZEALAND: BOX 3442, GPO, WELLINGTON

DEDICATED

To our daughter LaDonna and to her family, who have brought us so much joy, portraying in her life and pastoral ministry a living example and an exceptional role model of The Woman Believer. She has accepted the challenge and the opportunity of carrying the seeds of Biblical truth, enlightening her ever-expanding world of Christian ministry and of influence as a Biblical woman.

DAISY MARIE WASHBURN OSBORN

Bible Quotations in this book have been personalized, and sometimes synopsized, to encourage individual application. They are derived from The New King James Version and the Living Bible unless otherwise noted.

The Author

ISBN 0-87943-075-3

Copyright 1990 by Daisy Washburn Osborn

Printed in the United States of America

All Rights Reserved

Most Osborn books and cassettes are available at quantity discounts for bulk purchase to be used for gifts, resale, ministry outreaches, educational or other purposes.

For details write:

OSFO Publishers
Box 10
Tulsa, OK 74102 USA

CONTENTS

FOREWORD

WHEN I WAS A GIRL in a small church in Los Banos, California, a woman missionary from India dressed me in oriental attire and talked to me about committing my life as a missionary.

I am one of eleven children. My mother and one sister were tragically killed when I was only eight years old. I became a ward of the state and was fortunately placed under the guardianship of my oldest sister who raised me in a devoted Christian home.

My dream was to follow Christ and to become financially independent. I had already applied for and had been given employment by the leading department store in Los Banos, before I graduated from high school.

Then T.L. Osborn came along and we responded to each others signals. We fell in love, were married and entered full time ministry.

By the time I was 19 years old, I was co-pastor with T.L. of a new church in Portland, Oregon. When I was 20, we sailed for India. Our mission was not successful so we returned to the USA after only ten months.

That experience precipitated a crucial epoch in our lives as the Lord began to reveal Himself and to guide us into new beginnings.

Christ's Appearance

I persevered in my search for guidance to fulfill God's call upon my life. I experienced an awesome and miraculous visitation by Jesus Christ.

On the heels of that extraordinary encounter, I was given a shocking vision in which I was shown the female part of the body of Christ. It was personified by a single female figure — clean but destitute, alone and unattended, waiting alongside the roadway of life.

To my astonishment, that lonely and despairing woman cried out to me for help, for hope, for healing, for human dignity and for restoration in the functional body of Christ.

My Search Began

I began my spiritual search for God's woman, *The Woman Believer* — not for the Chinese or African or European or Asian or American woman. In our ministry around the world, I had observed all of these in life — all affected by varying cultures and differing national or religious customs. But my passionate search was for the woman whom God had created in His own image — His ideal for womanhood.

My search led me through the demoralizing labyrinth of cultures, of traditions and even of Judeo-Christian customs and theology, all of which have historically combined to circumscribe womankind within the limits of a second-class citizenry and of a subordinated personhood.

I never stopped in my penetrating search about womankind until I had laid a solid, Biblical foundation for helping women to discover conclusively that there is total salvation, divine dignity, quality self-esteem and unlimited ministry for women in the body of Christ on exactly the same redemptive basis as there is for men.

To share these vital discoveries, we have published this book, *The Woman Believer.*

Ministry to Millions

Around the world I have taught, preached and ministered, along with my husband, on the basis of total Biblical equality. My example has brought light and life and hope to millions of women. There is no doubt that I have ministered to more women, face to face, in more nations, than any woman who has ever lived.

I believe in practical faith and in positive ministry for women the same as for men. During more than four decades of ministry together, my husband and I have announced the gospel to great audiences in over 70 nations. These masses of people have been blessed and lifted by the teachings of Christ.

Heads of State, tribal kings, provincial commissioners, governors and national leaders have consistently numbered among our intimate friends.

My life's passion for many years has been to help women and girls — and people worldwide, to discover their individual dignity, their identity, their destiny, and their equality in God's redemptive plan.

It is my hope that *The Woman Believer* will help bring about that noble discovery wherever these chapters are read or taught.

Inclusive Language

Because this book is written to encourage women to see themselves in the scriptures, I have adapted Bible quotations so that they speak personally to *The Woman Believer* today.

Christ's promises are for female believers the same as they are for male believers. Therefore, a woman should read John. 14:12 like this: *She who believes in Me, the works that I do she will do also; and greater works than these she will do, because I go to My Father.*

It is vital that women read the scriptures this way since the purpose of the Bible is to speak God's message directly to the reader.

The literary style of English is traditionally masculinized — including the Bible. The neuter gender always becomes masculine. However we are taught to "understand" that both sexes are assumed to be included. But scholars agree that this presumption is no longer *apropos*.

To correct this literary insensibility to the female populace, prominent writers, media journalists and editors have adopted *inclusive* language because the academic and professional world has recognized the lingual inequity that has persisted.

For example, the Biblical Greek word *anthropos*, which has been translated man, usually means: *Human being without distinction of sex. Human individual. Every person. All people. Humans, distinct from animals, angels or God.*

This English word *man* has been used hundreds of times in the English Bible to translate Hebrew and Greek words which clearly mean both men and women, such as *ish* — individual, *adam* — human being, *enosh* — a mortal, *anthropos* — a human being, *tis* — someone, and numerous other words.

The Greek words *adelphos* and *adelphoi*, which have been translated into English as *brother* or *brethren*, are words that have been used scores of times where they clearly refer to both sexes. The accurate equivalent in English is *fellow believers, or Christians, or all believers; both male and female.*

Paul uses the term, *adelphos*, 130 times and it appears in the Acts over 80 times in which it means the sisters as well as the brothers.

Male–Female Language Bias

Nothing is more demeaning to human dignity than to be ignored. Women are generally disregarded in language by writers and by speakers — unless specifically referred to, whereas *man* and *mankind* are over-used terms in most vocabularies.

The literary world has faced this issue, adopting *inclusive* language that recognizes the dignity of female personhood. Christians should adopt these lingual patterns. All of our writings are published in *inclusive* language, as is *The Woman Believer.*

It is vitally important that women believers include themselves in the Bible. Masculinized language which is "intended" to mean both sexes, needs to be revised in today's world to make sure that *inclusive* terminology is used.

It has become *passé* for authors, journalists, editors or speakers to say *man* or *mankind* when they mean people of both sexes.

A very unscholarly and untactful habit prevails amidst writers and speakers alike. The word *man* is used almost consistently when a wide selection of other words could be used which would not only express the idea better, but would avoid monotony.

Rather than overtaxing the word *man,* one might say: People, humanity, humankind, persons, society, public, populace, men and women, mortals, everyone, everybody, souls, individuals, the world, human beings, inhabitants, human family, human race, folks, human community, *etc.*

It is curious to hear women speakers referring to people or to their present audience as *man* or *mankind,* even when speaking to an all-female assemblage.

It is no longer suitable in the *avant-garde* academic and literary world to say *man* or *he* and expect to be understood as including *woman* or *she. She* can no longer be ignored. The dignity of her personhood merits recognition.

We who are Christian speakers and writers, and who know that both women and men are created in God's image and who, therefore, esteem the unique value of each individual, should be the leaders, rather than the followers in language usage, and that is why *The Woman Believer* is presented in *inclusive* language.

INTRODUCTION

By T.L. Osborn

EVERY WOMAN on earth has unlimited possibilities in God. Redemption cannot be qualified sexually any more than it can be qualified economically, racially or socially.

Any woman or any man who becomes a new creature in Christ can become His co-worker and representative on any level of private or public ministry to which she or he feels led or called or inspired by Him to serve.

Women themselves, are the only persons who can limit Christ at work in their lives.

The Woman Believer is a woman who is created in God's image. Then she has been redeemed and reborn by His grace. She needs never permit sermonizers, ecclesiastics, doctrinaires, church traditions or social culture to negate her worth, to prevent her fulfillment, to impede her creativity, to stunt her objectives or to deprecate her standing as a redeemed daughter in God's royal family or as a qualified witness of Christ or as His representative and co-worker.

No believing woman needs to heed dictums or pronouncements made in the name of God, of the church, or of tradition, by clergymen who presume superiority over womankind by relegating them to a subordinate status in life and in the church.

These statements may controvert traditional theology. Often there is a super sensitivity to any logic that encourages women toward equality in public ministry. Reaction is sometimes spontaneous: Should not women be silent in the church? Is it not forbidden for them to teach? Are they not to be in submission to men? *Etc.*

Theological Manipulation

The male clergy has, through misconstruance of a few statements by Paul and Peter, greatly limited the international spread of the gospel by restraining and by impeding women believers from public ministry.

Scriptures taken out of their cultural context, and tarnished with tradition, have been contrived to demean and to repress the status of womanhood and her participation in public Christian ministry.

The normal criteria of human reasoning, of cultural rationale, of redemptive logistics, of historic synthesis, or of scientific or academic analysis would, if applied as in any other academic research, give intelligent balance to these few scriptures which have been traditionally so malconstrued. Without this scholarly rationale, the resulting prejudicial conclusions about women contradict the very principles of Christ's redemptive work which were revealed to and expounded by Paul.

Ordinary standards of scholastic enquiry have often been superseded by a kind of obfuscated supposition about women's role in life and in the church.

I have written this introduction hoping to motivate open-mindedness to redemptive truths which are presented in *The Woman Believer.*

If female readers can approach these chapters without the theological presumption that women are second-class Christians or that they are not qualified for public ministry, then God's spirit and His word can have the same freedom in their lives as in the lives of men believers.

Medieval Customs for Modern Culture?

In all of the New Testament there are only five cloistered notes of counsel in which Paul and Peter advised the new churches about women believers. These statements concerned their manner of dress, their hair styles, their adornment, their integration into the new Christian lifestyle and worship, their restrictions concerning learning and teaching, and their marital relationships.

Most of these verses address cultural *particulars* of a medieval epoch, and should never be construed as cultural *universals.*

These instructions were given to people of Biblical Middle Eastern societies and are impractical and inapplicable to women of modern culture who are educated, capable and experienced in every social, political, scientific, economic, professional and religious sphere of human life in this century.

The traditional patriarchal church has insisted on extracting these few episodic remarks concerning women who lived under the customs, rules and civic laws of ancient cultures, and has imperiously decreed them as dogmas for all women at all times. Societal rules applicable to that era have been turned into modern day anomalies.

Those guidelines for women of that epoch are not fixed standards for *The Woman Believer* of this century. Rather, they must be equated to the primitive and ofttimes pagan lifestyles and cultures of the epoch in which they were given.

A principal motive for these apostolic guidelines concerning women was to encourage obedience to civic laws.

Legal statutes of that epoch usually mandated that a wife was owned by her husband. But is that the legal status of a wife in developed nations? It was not even so among some of the societies where new converts were living then.

Roman law gave a man absolute control over his household and indisputable ownership of the family estate. Its codes and dictums legally restricted a woman to a subordinate role in the home and to unequivocal submission to her husband. But are these statutory laws incumbent upon women in progressive nations today?

Gentile Rules vs. Roman Laws

Among the varied societies, races, clans and communities which comprised the Roman Empire, some were even matriarchal. Many societal and cultural rules and gentile customs gave women varying degrees of legal authority, of property rights, of family jurisdiction and of economic prerogative and management initiative that were contradictory or even hostile to Roman laws.

In order to minimize the conflict between these gentile cultural family traditions and prevailing civic marital laws, Paul advised gentile converts to conform their family habits and marital relationships to the standards enforceable by Roman law — such as a husband's legal authority to demand the submission of his wife, and such as societal rules prohibiting women from any posture which might suggest authority — especially over a man, and which scrupulously dictated approved standards of dress, adornment and hair styles.

New gentile converts were urged to adapt their family lifestyles — and especially the dress and the conduct of women, to enforcable Roman laws and to community standards, not only to promote communal harmony, but more importantly, to avoid the suspicion and arrest of women believers by ruthless legal magistrates, army captains and soldiers who were under orders from Nero to obstruct, by every means possible, the spread of this vexatious "Jesus" cult.

Capturing, imprisoning, torturing and killing Christian women was Emperor Nero's most effective scheme to inhibit this spreading sect.

This is why Paul urged restraint on women from any public exposure which might appear immoderate or out of the ordinary, and which could thereby endanger their lives — such as when he told Timothy to not let women teach or show authority, but to be in silence and to adorn themselves modestly,[1] and such as when he urged the Colossian women to submit to their husbands.[2] It was very important that they respect Roman laws and that they conform their lives accordingly.

But are these menacing political conditions and civic laws which early believers lived under, applicable to Christian believers in free, progressive societies today? Should those restraints be imposed upon educated women believers in this epoch?

Medieval Customs for Men

Scriptures concerning the cultural practices of men in Bible times are considered irrelevant or inappropriate to believing men today — unless they happen to coincide with current male customs and practices.   The same logistics apply to today's female world.

To restrict educated, professional, modern women to inferior roles of silence and submission in church ministry among politically free, modern societies today, gives the impression that the Bible is a repressive and obsolete book for women.

To impose outdated restraints upon modern women is no different than the practice of cloistered holiness movements that dictate the use of horses and buggies because they reject electronic and mechanical progress.

Biblical standards for women usually correspond to similar principles for men. Why have these patterns concerning women been imposed as binding for all time while instructions concerning

men are understood to relate only to the epoch in
which they were expressed?

Archaic Inequities

The Woman Believer in today's world under-
stands the irrelevancy of these ancient restraints
upon her life in modern society. She can no longer
allow herself to be manacled or muzzled by religious maxims which are *passé* in every other sector
of contemporary society.

Present-day church traditions do not usually
impose upon modern women the dress and hair
styles advocated in 1 Timothy 2:9-12 and 1 Peter
3:1-6, nor the head-covering of 1 Corinthians 11:3-6
which bore great significance in that primitive
culture. Prostitutes went about with uncovered
heads, but the Christian woman's head-covering
distinguished her from the promiscuous female.

The admonitions of Paul and of Peter which
were appropriate to their societal and political
structures are not applicable for today's culture.
They were urging obedience to enforceable civic
laws and to prevailing customs. But those factors
have changed in today's world.

The headship of man and the mutual submission
of husbands and wives, emphasized to the young
converts from those pagan cultures (1 Co. 11:3-6;
Ep. 5:21-25), were carefully compared with how
Christ relates to His church — as its source and in
sacrificial love. These remarks were never
intended to sequester women in marital situations of
indignity, disrespect, disloyalty or physical abuse.
Christ never relates to His church in such ways.

Apostolic Epoch vs. Today's Society

It is logical that, in the light of their civil and political climate, women in the first century were well advised to be silent in public worship and not to teach. The Christian-hating emperor, Nero, notoriously captured women believers, exploited them, and publicly tortured and killed them in order to obstruct the spread of the new "Christian" cult. Women needed to exercise extreme caution in public, in order to avoid vengeful arrest. Female believers were taken into custody on the basis of bare suspicion. They were the emperor's choice target for bringing shame, fear and punishment upon the despised "Christian" sect.

But as I said before, such an antagonistic environment does not menace *The Woman Believer* in progressive societies today.

Many cultural influences, rules and laws affected early Christian households, business patterns and forms of worship. Though not detailed in the Biblical text, scholars are well aware that apostolic instructions about women and households must be weighed and balanced in the light of Hebrew and Gentile practices, religious rules and civil laws of that epoch.

How unfair to pluck a few remarks made by Paul or Peter about women in primitive cultures, and to manipulate them in order to silence, subjugate, sequester, stifle, suppress and subordinate over half of the body of Christ, limiting them in their ministries as His witnesses. Such obvious bias can no longer be tolerated by the thinking Christian of this epoch.

Numerous other aspects of medieval culture and tradition bear upon the Pauline admonitions concerning women. His words are not to be lifted out of their cultural context and used to impose outdated restraints upon *The Woman Believer* of this century.

I have written this introduction in the hope that these observations will encourage believing women to allow Christ and His word to have full expression through their lives, *actually becoming all that God has had in mind for* (them) *to be.*[3]

1.   1 Ti.2:9-12
2.   Col. 3:18
3.   Ro.5:2 LB

PART I

JESUS REVEALED
IN
WOMEN

EACH WOMAN who receives Christ becomes another expression of God in human flesh. "Christian" to a woman means being Christ–like in the fullest possible measure.

We cannot see Christ, so we cannot express our love to Him, but we can see people, so we can do to them what we would like to do to Christ if we could see Him.

When a dead baby was thrust into my arms by a frantic mother, Jesus in me was moved with compassion and a miracle resulted. Never underestimate what the Lord will do through you as you discover Jesus revealed in you.

- Serving Jesus is serving people.
- Loving God is loving people.
- Exalting the Lord is lifting people.
- Touching Christ is touching people.

You mark yourself as a special woman of God and as His partner in lifting and in blessing humanity when you make the vital discovery of recognizing and of identifying Jesus at work in and through you. In that way you truly discover *The Woman Believer*.

Chapter 1

GOD'S BIG IDEA

GOD CAME TO this world in the form of a human person — Jesus Christ. He came to reveal Himself to women and to men alike.

Religion had distorted the concept of what God was like. So He revealed Himself in human form in order that people could understand Him and relate to Him as a living reality in their own lives.

People touched God when they touched Christ. They saw God when they saw Jesus. He said: *The one who has seen Me has seen the Father.*[1]

The big idea which Jesus brought to this world — the idea which totally upset the religious system of His day, was identifying Himself with God as His Father, and Himself as God's child.

Religion was so unprepared for this concept that the theological hierarchy never stopped until they succeeded in having Jesus crucified as a heretic and an impostor. Their railing accusation: *He said that God was His FATHER, making Himself equal with God.*[2]

They did not realize that God's idea from the beginning was to reproduce Himself in human form — both male and female, as His own offspring.

God in Human Form

In the beginning, when God created the first human person, He breathed His divine breath of life into that form of clay, and it became a living soul — in the image and in the likeness of God. God reproduced Himself in human flesh.

But Adam and Eve were seduced by Satan, God's enemy. As a result they denied the word of God and His integrity. God, who is love, could not overlook this lack of trust. His plan to have them as His friends and partners was thwarted by the deceit of Satan. *The soul who sins shall die.*[3]

Adam and Eve sinned and therefore had to be separated from God. The process of degeneration so affected human history that people lost the concept of God as their Father and of themselves as His offspring. But God never gave up on His big idea.

To restore this relationship, God sent Jesus, His Son, in human flesh, to redemonstrate His original concept — to reveal what He is like. The life of Jesus revealed to us what God's dream is like for every woman and for every man.

But since sin had separated us from God, we had to be redeemed from our sins, and restored to God before He could live in us and express Himself through us as He had planned. That is why Christ assumed our guilt and suffered all the penalty of judgment for our sins, so that we could be redeemed to God as though no sin had ever been committed.

Christ was without sin.[4]   Therefore, being innocent, He could assume our guilt and endure our punishment. He died in our place.[5] His blood was shed for the remission of our sins.

The Bible tells us that whoever believes that fact is justified before God and is accepted by Him.[6]

As believers, women and men have been redeemed, justified and restored to God[7] as though no sin had ever been committed.[8] By believing on Christ, they can be re-born into God's family[9] as His children, and become His expressions in this world.

Since Christ has paid for our sins and has restored us to God, He now wills to live in every person who receives Him in her or his life by faith.   He wills to express Himself to others through women and men, without being restricted or limited or hindered by human race, color, social status, or sex, because all human persons are created in His image, designed to be His expressions and His co-workers.

Each woman who receives Christ becomes another expression of God in human flesh. "Christian" to a woman, means being Christ-like in the fullest possible measure.

Jesus Christ does not change, nor is He limited when He comes to live in a woman believer.

1.	Jn.14:9	5.	Is.53:5	7.	Ro.5:1;6:16-18
2.	Jn.5:18		2Co.5:21		Re.5:9
3.	Eze.18:4,20		Ro.6:8-10	8.	Col.1:22 LB; 2:13-15 LB
4.	He.4:15	6.	Ro.5:1	9.	Ga.4:4-7 LB
			1Co.6:11		
			Ac.10:35		
			Ep.1:6-7		

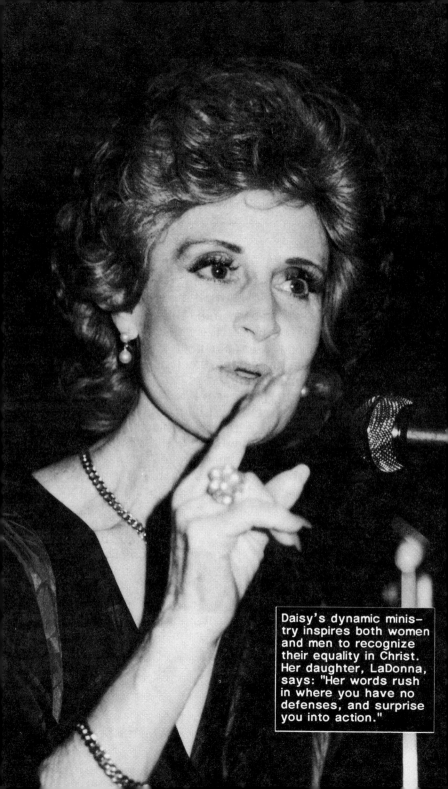

Daisy's dynamic ministry inspires both women and men to recognize their equality in Christ. Her daughter, LaDonna, says: "Her words rush in where you have no defenses, and surprise you into action."

Chapter 2

GOD ALIVE IN WOMEN TOO

GOD'S DREAM FOR every woman on earth is to be able to live in and through her. He created her in His own likeness — in His own image.[1] Each woman is the divine creation of God — made for God to dwell in and to express Himself through. God's total love plan is to make it possible for any human person to be like Jesus.

As a friend and as a partner with God in carrying out His plan on earth, the most vital discovery for *The Woman Believer* is to learn the life-changing facts about Jesus revealed in women, and to realize that He now wills to do His works through women the same as through men. Christ is no more limited by the sex than He is by the race of His followers today.

That is why when any woman receives Christ, all that He does *to* her, He then wants to do *through* her. He becomes flesh in her. By receiving Christ, she can then be a channel through which He blesses those around her who need His help. He functions through her as His body.

This is why our Lord told us, in Matthew 25:34-36, that He wants us to feed the hungry, to give drink to the thirsty, to clothe the naked and to visit the sick and the prisoners. He underscored the fact that *inasmuch as we do it to one of the least of these, we do it to Him. (v.40)*

Our Lord says to every woman believer whose life is committed to Him in loving service and ministry to people:

"When I had no home, you shared yours.

"When I had no clothes, you gave me yours.

"When I was tired, you helped me find a place to rest.

"When I was afraid, you gave me assurance.

"When I was alone, you were my friend.

"When I was in jail, you came to my cell.

"When I was sick, you nursed me back to health.

"When I lost my job, you helped me find work.

"When I was aged, you made me feel needed.

"When I was mocked, you stood by my side.

"When I sorrowed, you shared my grief.

"When I was happy, you laughed with me."

Jesus expresses Himself through believing women exactly the same as He does through believing men. He is no more limited by their sex than He is by their race.

1.   Ge.1:27

Chapter 3

THE MARKED WOMAN

YOU MARK YOURSELF as a special woman of God and as Christ's partner in lifting and blessing people, when you make the vital discovery of recognizing and of identifying Him, liberated in and through you.

Mother Teresa of Calcutta, India says: "By getting in touch with people, we find God. Because we cannot see Christ, we cannot express our love to Him; but our neighbors we can always see, and we can do to them what, if we saw Christ, we would like to do to Him.

"Our works are only an expression of our love for Christ. Our hearts need to be full of love for Him and since we have to express that love in action, naturally then (people) are the means of expressing our love for God."

She adds, and I agree: "It is not the poor who are indebted to us but we who are indebted to them. They make it possible for us to serve God."

I love the words of a song I heard recently:

Jesus said, when you love someone
In my Name, you're loving Me.
Jesus said, when you touch someone
In my Name, you're touching Me.
Jesus said, when you reach someone
In my Name, you're reaching Me.

I have learned the priceless lesson that I am ministering to Christ when I minister to people.

Mother With Dead Child

At a national women's conference abroad, a mother came to me with an unbearable hurt. Her baby daughter had died. She shoved the little baby into my arms.

What a helpless feeling, that is — unless you identify with Jesus in your life. You never know what you will do under any given circumstance. But when you practice living the Jesus-life, then you will be a Jesus-person regardless of the situation.

After reaching out, in my heart, to God for His guidance, and with the little body held close to mine, I began to pray. I knew the Lord wanted to show His compassion, so I rebuked death and commanded life to come back into the child's body, in the name of Jesus. Then I waited as I walked back and forth, holding the baby close to my bosom.

Suddenly I felt a quiver go through the baby's body and I knew its life had returned. I just held her close to me, as I quietly walked about. Before long I was able to present the child back to her mother, restored and completely healed.

Never underestimate what Jesus Christ will do through you as you identify with Him at work in and through you. When you do, you discover what real fulfillment is in life. You mark yourself as a true Jesus-woman.

The Woman Believer in Action

Because we have Christ's nature in us, He wills to do the same things through us that He did when He was on this earth. *Jesus Christ is the same yesterday and today and forever.*[1]

Every woman has the right to choose to allow the Lord Jesus to be the same in and through her today, as He was in Bible days.

No literate woman believer should allow obsolete dogmas of primitive ecclesiasticisms to limit or restrain or muzzle or silence the Christ who lives in her.

1.   He.13:8

Daisy and her husband, T.L. Osborn, share as teammates in their ministry to millions around the world.

Chapter 4

OUR MISSION TO MILLIONS

SERVING JESUS is serving people. Loving God is loving people. Exalting our Lord is lifting people. Touching Christ is touching people.

God is Spirit. You as a woman, are His flesh, His visibility, His touchability, His accessibility, His tangibility — His reality in life. He is revealed in and through you as a woman believer exactly the same as He is revealed in and through a man who is a believer.

For over four rich decades, I have dedicated my life (and I continue to do so) to reach out to hurting, neglected, despairing, lonely, forsaken human persons, most of whom have lived their lives without ever having heard about salvation through Christ. God loves people, needs them and values them so much that He gave His Son to redeem them to Himself, so that they may become His intimate friends and partners in life.

As a woman believer and as a follower of Christ, I have ministered to multitudes of beautiful people, face to face, in over 70 nations.

I have chosen to allow Christ to function in and through me despite any disparagement or demeaning voices which might question the validity of my position or of my achievements in public ministry. Christ's expression through human persons is no more affected by one's sex than it would be by one's race or color or academic or social or economic status.

There is no life so rich for a woman and no reward so fulfilling to her as to discover the vital lesson of Jesus revealed in women.

When woman discovers that truth, she has learned one of life's most significant lessons — one which constantly keeps her experiencing dynamic fulfillment in life. She has truly become what I call *The Woman Believer* today.

PART II

YOUR CHOICE POWER

GRIEF OR HAPPINESS, apprehension or confidence, delight or discontent, action or passive submission, is a choice that YOU make.

I say, *Religion* gave birth to twins:

One is called *Culture;*
The other is called *Tradition.*

These twins often keep women from becoming what God designed them and redeemed them to be.

Choose to practice the awareness of Jesus alive in you.

You learn by teaching. You gain by giving. You reap by sowing. You grow by sharing.

Your choice power as a woman, puts you in control of your own destiny, and guarantees that you can become all that you choose to let Christ become in you, *The Woman Believer.*

Chapter 5

A DREAMER — AN ACHIEVER

THE FOLLOWING Amanda Bradley phrases reflect my life's goal and they portray the way that I live.

Lord, let me be a dreamer and let me be a doer.
Let me strive and steadily achieve.

Let me be a learner and let me be a teacher.
Let me give and graciously receive.

Let me be your follower. Let me be your friend.
Let me hear Your voice and heed Your call.

Let me know the plans you have for me.
Let me, by Your strength, fulfill them all.

To realize true fulfillment in life, you must discover your choice power and take charge of your own life as *The Woman Believer* that you are.

Have you ever wondered why some women are negative? And why others are positive? Why some systematically fail? And why others consistently succeed?

Why do some women act? Why do others only react? Why do some depend upon the opinions of friends? Why do others trust their own opinions?

You Are Included

In the Bible, Paul writes to women as well as to men:

Through Christ, all the kindness of God has been poured out upon us ... and now He is sending us (women) out around the world to tell all people everywhere the great things God has done for them, so that they, too, will believe and obey Him.[1]

So now, since we (women) have been made right in God's sight by faith in His promises ... Christ has brought us into this place of highest privilege where we now stand. And we look with confidence and joy. Because ... we can actually become all that God has had in His mind for us to be.[2]

We have published this vital book, *The Woman Believer*, to help you as a woman — or a man, to become all that God designed you to be, and to help you to discover how your choice power determines your fulfillment in life.*

1.   Ro.1:5 LB
2.   Ro.5:1-2 LB

*For further inspiration, read my book, *Five Choices for Women Who Win.*

Chapter 6

CHOOSING TO BE POSITIVE

AS A YOUNG COUPLE, my husband, T.L. Osborn and I went to India as missionaries. In route, I read Aimee Semple McPherson's story.

In her youth, Aimee and her husband had gone to China as missionaries. Both he and their little son had become very ill. Finally she buried her husband in China and returned home as a nineteen-year-old widow.

I marvel that only the sad facts of Aimee's life impressed me. She had so many positive and triumphant experiences. But her becoming a widow in China and her coming home alone with her baby, was what I pondered deeply.

Perhaps it was because I was a young wife and mother in route to India with my husband, and I secretly feared a similar fate. I had not learned about my choice power and how dynamically it affected my life. I was choosing to think negatively, instead of positively. I lived with apprehension, instead of confidence and sure enough, my husband almost died of typhoid fever. My fears almost materialized.

Bitter Or Better

People's attitudes — negative or positive, have to do with their choices.

Grief or happiness, apprehension or confidence, delight or discontent is a choice you make. Right now, you are determining how this book is affecting your life.

In each experience, you have the choice of becoming better or bitter; fearful or confident, haughty or humble; hateful or grateful; constructive or destructive.

Always choose a positive attitude. Never be afraid. Exercise your ability to decide to be on God's side. As you choose to be all that God wants you to be, you will discover that it is really His choice being expressed through you, and that is the secret of true, lasting happiness and fulfillment in life.

You Are Distinguished

Life may seem easier for you as a woman, if you move with the crowd, or if you yield to what others think you should be or do, or if you compromise your convictions to suit the opinions of society. But remember, Jesus looks at you as a unique individual — as a distinguished person.

T.L. and I pioneered mass evangelism all over the world. We were the first couple to go to non-Christian nations, to use large fields, parks, race courses or stadiums and amass 20,000 to 250,000 people of various religions, proclaiming the Gospel of the risen Christ and expecting Him to confirm Himself alive by signs, wonders and miracles as He did in Bible days.[1]

We learned never to look at the multitude, but

to be conscious of the human individuals that comprise that mass of people.

As we minister to those enormous crowds, we take great courage in knowing that God sees each individual and is concerned with each person. And you can take courage too in knowing that He is concerned with you as the unique person that you are.

Regardless of what others do, since God designed you as one-of-a-kind, you can choose to be different from the crowd — to be all that God wants you to be.

It is not always easy to fulfill God's plan for your life. You must continually make positive choices, based on the fact that you are identified with Him. Culture and tradition cannot pour you into their mold when you choose to be the person God created you to be — *The Woman Believer*.

1.   Mk.16:20

Daisy Osborn's private library contains rare treasures of knowledge to help womankind achieve the dignity of success.

Chapter 7

TRANSCENDING CULTURAL ROLES

I SOMETIMES SAY that *Religion* gave birth to twins. One was called *Culture,* and the other *Tradition.* These twins of religion often keep women from becoming what God wants them to be — and this is a tragedy for *The Woman Believer.*

Every person has obstacles to overcome which result from roles established for them by culture and religion. Girls and boys are cast into societal or cultural roles from the time they are born.

God does not slot people into limiting roles.*

I am Daisy Washburn Osborn. I am blessed because I am married to T.L. Osborn. We are sweethearts, we are friends, we are companions, spouses, and intimate teammates.

Being a wife, a mother, a grandmother and a great-grandmother does not change who I am — Daisy Marie Washburn Osborn, the unique individual that God created.

The role that society prescribes for me does not dictate or limit my functions in God's plan for me.

---

* For further discussion about a no limits woman, read my book, *Woman Without Limits.*

It may not be easy for a woman to be all that God wants her to be, but if she has enough faith, enough love, enough courage, and enough trust in God and enough love for Him, she can succeed because of her choice power.

A woman can surmount any difficulty or accomplish anything she believes God wills for her, and she can do it with dignity and with grace as *The Woman Believer*.

A Woman Ahead of Her Time

Maria Woodworth-Etter (1844-1924) was a woman ahead of her time.

Saved when she was 12 years old, Maria heard the voice of Jesus saying, "Go out and gather lost sheep." But in the late 1800's the church did not allow women to preach the gospel. So Maria told the Lord, "When I grow up, I'll marry a missionary (the church allowed women to do that); then I'll serve You."

But God's plan for Maria was not limited by the religious dogmas of her day. He never gave up on His dream for her, and Maria finally said, "Yes."

That remarkable woman preached the gospel until she was 80 years old, despite incredible opposition. And that was before the epoch of political rhetoric about the constitutional rights of women. The church and the public had no tolerance for a woman preacher.

But Maria succeeded in becoming what God

wanted her to be.

She exercised her choice power. She chose to obey God instead of man or culture or tradition.

That brave, diminutive lady proclaimed the gospel in packed auditoriums and in huge overflowing tents all over this nation — a dynamic example of *The Woman Believer* in action with Christ.

God never changes in His ideal for human persons. When elders or bishops or pontificates try to barricade progress and change, He just gets a new generation and keeps unfolding His dream.

It was Maria Woodworth-Etter's day then, and she used her choice power, fulfilling God's dream for her life. But this is your day — your turn to activate your choice power as a woman, by becoming what God designed you to be, despite tradition and culture that raises barriers along your road to greater achievement through Christ.

Daisy believes a successful teacher is an avid student. She says, "No one learns everything, but everyone can learn something. Once you have knowledge then you can impart it to someone else."

Chapter 8

5 QUESTIONS FOR WOMEN IN GOD'S PLAN

HERE ARE FIVE important questions which concern your choice power.

Question No. 1.
WHY use your choice power?

The priority of the Church — of each believer — is to share Christ with people. Is this your priority?

Ask yourself these questions, and see if reaching people is what you give precedence to: What do I do with my money? With my time? With my talents?

If you find that you are not engaged to some degree in God's most important work, you can turn around and choose today to experience the greatest possible happiness, by being part of His plan for people.

Question No. 2.
WHO should use their choice power?

The greatest opportunity for every believer, regardless of race, color, economic status, education or sex, is to share Christ with people. That is ultimate happiness — ultimate achievement for *The Woman Believer.*

You do not need to ask God to send you to China. Choose to begin where you are. Share Christ with your family, your neighborhood, your community, your town, your state, your nation. Keep reaching out and you may reach your way to China. Once you begin, doors will keep opening.

The principle is:

> When you know Christ, you share Christ.

> When you receive life, you impart life.

> When you are healed, you heal others.

> When you are blessed, you are a blessing.

> When you are forgiven, you give forgiveness.

> When you accept love, you express love.

That is *The Woman Believer* in essence. The choice is yours — now.

That is the lifestyle of a believer. The key is awareness. Practice being aware of Jesus alive and at work in and through you, making you all that God planned for you to be.

When you look at someone, remember to say to yourself: "Jesus is in me. He is seeing this individual through my eyes, because He has no eyes but mine."

God's arms reach out to hurting, needy people when your arms are extended. His arms are your arms. And He does His reaching and His touching through you, *The Woman Believer.*

Christ chose you and me to do His work. You can choose the opportunity of working with Him, which is the happiest life on earth.

Yes! Success, happiness, achievement and progress are all realized through your choice power as a woman.

Question No. 3.
WHERE can you use your choice power?

Anywhere you are in your world — the world that surrounds you. Your world needs your influence. In your world of influence where you live, you have the power to choose what you will do with your life.

Your influence has tremendous creative power in your world, because you have the power to create around you the kind of world you want. That power is seed-power and it is your choice power that determines the kind of seed that you plant. With the seed of your thoughts, of your words and of your actions, you influence the people of your world.

When Jesus is at the center of your world, then your seed-power, positively exercised, creates a beautiful world around you.

Choose every opportunity to be what God wants you to be.

From Smuggling to Witnessing

A family of drug smugglers came to Christ in a meeting where we were ministering. They had been in prison for smuggling cocaine across the border. The family had developed a million dollar drug business.

The wife, her husband, their children, her husband's brother, their father and mother, father-in-law and mother-in-law, uncles, aunts, cousins — the entire family accepted Jesus Christ as they heard the gospel.

I counseled them, "Do not lose your ability to smuggle. Now you have something worth bringing to people." I told them that a big percent of the world cannot receive the gospel unless believers are willing to risk their own freedom to carry it to the people, as the early Christians did — often in circumstances where their actions were in violation of existing laws and customs.

I told them what Jesus said: *This gospel will be preached in all the world as a witness to all the nations, and then the end will come.*[1]

That family of "smugglers" was greatly encouraged to hear me tell them that God had a plan for their talents. I helped them to focus on utilizing their abilities to carry the right substance — the gospel of Christ.

That is how God accepts people — including

you. He takes you where you are and makes your life into something beautiful for people. And that is the fruit of your choice power.

You Have the Power to Begin

The gospel must first be published to all the nations.[2] That is why we have printed literature by the tons and have distributed it around the world, in 132 different languages. We started with just one language, but we kept expanding to others, because we made a choice to involve ourselves in God's dream for people of many nations.

You also have the power to choose to become what God wants you to be.

Do you feel that you are not ready to launch out? My counsel is, just begin. You are ready for the first step now, and you will become ready for tomorrow's challenges by the steps you take today.

You will learn by teaching.

You will gain by giving.

You will reap by sowing.

You will grow by sharing.

This is God's formula for your success and fulfillment. By choosing to be part of God's love-plan for people, you are fulfilling God's ultimate dream for *The Woman Believer*.

You Have Authority

Only women can change the world of women, and there are many more women than men in the world today. Perhaps two-thirds of all believers in the church are women. That is why *inclusive* language is so important for pastors, teachers, church leaders and evangelists to use.

Joel prophesied, *And it shall come to pass in the last days, says God, that I will pour out of My Spirit upon all flesh; And your sons and your daughters shall prophesy ... And on My menservants and on My maidservants I will pour out My Spirit in those days, and they shall prophesy.*[3]

God is fulfilling that prophecy today as women discover their choice power to be all that God designed and redeemed them to be.

You do not need anyone's permission to obey Christ or to allow the Holy Spirit to carry out the Lord's ministry through you. You have been given your commission by the highest authority.[4]

Remember that church dogmas, dictums and traditions which restrict or restrain women from public ministry have no power or authority over you or over your ministry as a woman believer, unless you give that power and authority to them.

Aimee Semple McPherson, Maria Woodworth-Etter, Sojourner Truth, myself, and a great host of other women have consistently chosen to refuse to allow the patriarchal church hierarchy to limit our ministries. We, and so many other brave women of God, have succeeded because Jesus Christ has been honored in our lives as Lord. It is He who has called us. It is His word that we have trusted. It is He who has ordained us. It is His anointing which has equipped us and has confirmed us.

You have been commissioned by Jesus Christ. Do not wait for a council of elders, or of pastors, or of priests, or of cardinals to tell you what you can or cannot do. Act in Christ's name as *The Woman Believer* that you are.

Watch Yourself Grow

Any woman who sees her identity in Jesus Christ is one who has discovered her personal choice power in life. She is a peacemaker. She is humble. She is willing to serve anyone, anytime, anywhere. That kind of service is the greatest kind of leadership, and it is the only true road to real happiness and achievement.

Look at what you have, at what you know, at what you can do. Do not look at what you do not have, or at what you do not know, or at what you cannot do.

Do what you can do. Give what you can give. Be what you are. Share what you know. And watch yourself grow.

Jesus said, in essence: "To be the greatest in the kingdom of God, be a believer, a follower of Me, a disciple, and then graduate with My highest degree of honor: Be a servant to all."[5]

For *The Woman Believer*, there are no limits. The greatest opportunities in ministry are yours to choose — those of simply helping people. That opens the whole world to you. Look at what that basic commitment has led to in the life of Mother Teresa of Calcutta.

Question No. 4.
WHEN do you use your choice power?

Today. There have never before been as many people living on the earth. There have never before been as many needs to fill or as many problems to solve. There have never before been as many lost people to help.

We have never before had so much technology or so much equipment at our disposal. There have never before been so many facilities that we can utilize, so much knowledge at our disposal, so many open doors, and so much encouragement.

Now is the time for you to decide to be part of God's plan and to begin to recognize and to use your choice power as *The Woman Believer* that you are.

The harvest is great. The opportunities within your reach are unlimited, but the laborers — especially women laborers, are few.

God needs you. You are unique and important. No one else can do the job that He has for you to do — and the time is short.

Choose today to be part of God's plan.

Question No. 5.
HOW do you use your choice power?

The first step is to get right with God. Discover God's idea for you. You can only choose God's best when you are right with Him. That is how you become *The Woman Believer* that God designed you to be.

When you have chosen to be on His side and united with Him, that opens the door for you to experience the true joy of being the woman He wants you to be.

He says, *Your cry came to Me at a favorable time, when the doors of welcome were wide open.*[6]

Today you can choose to accept the life that Christ offers you. He loves you and He desires only good for you. Believe on the Lord Jesus Christ and be born again as you choose to take these five wonderful steps in faith.

Five Steps to Become
The Woman Believer

I

The first step is: Recognize that sin has poisoned human nature. Accept the fact that everyone *must,* therefore, *be born again.*[7] *All have sinned and fall short of God's glorious ideal.*[8]

Sin separates you from God.[9]

II

The second step is: Repent, and be sorry for your sins.

Unless you repent you will perish.[10]   And remember, *God so loved the world, that He gave His only begotten Son, that whoever believes in Him should not perish, but have everlasting life.*[11]

III

The third step is: Confess your sins to God.

Whoever covers their sins will not prosper, but whoever confesses and forsakes them will have mercy.[12]

If we confess our sins, God is faithful and just to forgive us our sins and to cleanse us from all unrighteousness.[13]

IV

The fourth step is: Ask God to forgive you of every sin you have ever committed.

In Jesus Christ we have redemption through His blood, the forgiveness of sins, according to the riches of His grace.[14]

V

And the fifth step is: Receive Jesus as your Savior.

For if you tell others with your own mouth that

Jesus Christ is your Lord, and believe in your own heart that God has raised Him from the dead, you will be saved.[15]

You can make contact with Jesus right now.

Prayer

Pray this prayer. And remember: Praying is simply talking to God, who is your loving heavenly Father. He receives you as His child — right now.

Say this:

Thank You, Lord Jesus, for what You have done for me on the cross.

You bore my sin, You bore my sickness, You took my problems, You have given me Your righteousness.

You have given me Your health, and You have given me Your solutions.

I repent of my sins. Forgive every wrong I have ever done.

I receive Your love and Your forgiveness. I welcome You into my life as my Lord and Savior. I believe that you have redeemed me.

Now that You live in me, my body is holy and I accept Your health.

I choose to be Your ambassador to my world. Now You can see with my eyes, You can hear with my ears, You can speak with my lips, You can

smile with my face, You can think with my mind, You can embrace with my arms, and You can walk with my feet.

Make me all that you want me to be. From this day, I will go forward with faith and love and confidence, aware that You are alive in me and at work through me.

I use my choice power today by receiving You into my heart. And I thank You, Jesus, for my new life.

Amen.

1.	Mt.24:14	5.	Mt.20:27	10.	Lu.13:5
2.	Mk.13:10		Mt.23:11	11.	Jn.3:16
3.	Ac.2:17-18	6.	2Co.6:2 LB	12.	Pr.28:13
4.	Mk.16:15	7.	Jn.3:7	13.	1Jn.1:9
	Jn.14:12	8.	Ro.3:23 LB	14.	Ep.1:7
	Ac.1:8	9.	Is.59:2	15.	Ro.10:9 LB

PART III

MY
POSITIVE
CHOICE

WHEN I WAS SIXTEEN years old I attended an evangelistic meeting near our home. There I met a young musician and youth-preacher, seventeen-year old Tommy Osborn.

My choice to go with my husband wherever God would lead us could have been a traumatic experience for me in the light of the turbulent years of my early life.

I had looked forward to motherhood. But our little daughter only lived a few days.

Then came the challenge to go to India as missionaries, but we could not give proof of the gospel.

Jesus appeared to my husband. I had to make a major choice myself. I would not trade those suitcases today for the loveliest house in the world. I am truly a fulfilled woman.

Chapter 9

MY OPTIONS AS A WOMAN

TRADITIONALLY I WAS taught that a wife's place is by the side of her husband, and that a mother's place is at home with her children. So, as a young mother with two children, and as the wife of a world missionary-evangelist, I faced some crucial decisions.

I could remain in a comfortable home, sending our children to school and offering them a normal lifestyle. Or I could go with my husband, as his team-mate in ministry, moving from country to country and from city to city, making life for our children as normal as possible, on the road and on the go.

Neither God nor my husband could choose for me. It was a decision that I had to make. I chose to go!

Our home base is Tulsa, Oklahoma, but cities around the globe have been our residence. Our children's classroom was always wherever we happened to be at school time. I was their teacher. The world was their playground.

No woman who ever lived has had the privileges afforded me during my adult life. I have taught, preached and ministered with my husband in over 70 countries as we have conducted mass evangelism crusades of Bible faith worldwide. I have shared every trial and enjoyed every triumph through over four remarkable decades of international ministry. I have witnessed the opening of blind eyes; I have seen cripples rise and walk; I have encouraged mothers with their helpless children and watched them go away rejoicing as their little ones were made whole. I have seen the weary people beam with delight, and I have wept with the suffering who have been healed by Christ our Lord.

Turbulent Childhood

My choice to go with my husband wherever God would lead us could have been a traumatic experience for me in the light of the turbulent years of my early life.

When I was only eight years old my mother and one sister were killed in a tragic train-car accident. One of my brothers had died. The remaining nine children were scattered from one place to another. My father was unable to provide for and to maintain a home for us in Merced, California.

When I was small, my mother had taken me to Sunday School, but my first real awareness of Christianity and God came to me while living with my oldest sister. At the age of twelve, I publicly accepted Jesus as my personal Savior.

Chapter 10

EARLY CHOICES OF DESTINY

AT THE AGE of sixteen, I attended an evangelistic meeting near our home. There I met a young musician and youth-preacher, seventeen-year-old Tommy Osborn.

We were married at very young ages. Shortly afterwards, we embarked on our first evangelistic journey into the Kiamichi Mountains of Oklahoma. The venture almost ended in tragedy because I nearly died from food poisoning. My young, believing husband prayed fervently and I was healed. We were so glad to be able to come out of those backward mountains and to get back to Tulsa. We had an old Model "A" Ford. We arrived in Tulsa on three tires and one rim.

Then came our decision to "go west." So with very little money we made our journey back to sunny California. My husband took a part-time job while we looked for an open door of ministry. A church called us for a "revival" so we traded the old car for train tickets to that church, and have been going ever since.

More Tragedy

I had looked forward to motherhood and it was a blessed event. But our little daughter only lived a week. This left us feeling very much alone and in a sense of deep despair.

By God's grace we buried our sorrowful experience in service to others.

A decision to pioneer a new church in Portland, Oregon uprooted us once more. We took an old barn-type building with less than a dozen people who had formed a Bible class. Within a short time, that old building was packed with people coming from near and far to see what God was doing through our young lives.

Then came the challenge to go to India as missionaries. By this time a little son had blessed our marriage. So, with our ten-month-old boy, packed trunks and hearts full of hope and pioneer zeal, we sailed to India.

Our missionary term of ministry was to be five years, but in less than a year we were forced to return home. Those months in India were some of the most harassing of my life. My young husband lingered between life and death for six weeks with typhoid fever. Our little son fought for his life when stricken with cholera and amoebic dysentery.

But our most difficult challenge was our inability to succeed in ministry.

When we tried to convince the people of India that Jesus is God's Son, that He is risen from the dead, and that He is the only way to eternal life, they were unimpressed.

We felt defeated, discouraged and disheartened. We sold our five-year stock of clothing and sup-

plies, and managed enough money to get back on our
feet in America.

The Challenge of Choice

Broken in health and in spirit, but glad to be
home once again, my husband made me a promise.
With deep emotion he said, "Sweetheart, I will
never again take you away from the shores of our
beloved country."

Very soon we were again pastoring a growing
church congregation and our lives had begun to
normalize again. We were settled in as pastors
and we now had two children. But soon, our
missionary dreams blossomed anew and I faced
another crisis in my life as a mother.

This decision could not be a casual one.
Something had happened to my husband. He saw
the Lord in a vision. We had been praying, fasting
and believing God to give us the answer to why we
had not succeeded in India. Christ's commission
had told us to go, but we could not give proof of
the gospel to those precious Indian people.

When Jesus appeared to my husband, He gave
him the answer to the dilemma we had faced, and
told him to go to the peoples of the world, assuring
him that signs, wonders and miracles would confirm the gospel and that multitudes would be saved
as a result.

It was during these days that I sought God concerning specific direction for my own life. The
Lord made me to realize that I had to make a
major choice myself. The man whom I had taken

to be my husband was determined to obey God and to go anywhere in the world in his quest to win souls to Christ.

A whole new world had opened up to us. Mighty signs and miracles began to take place in our meetings and we knew that this was the answer — the secret to successful missionary evangelism among the world's unreached millions.

My husband said, "Honey, now we know how to convince people that Christ is risen! Jesus was approved by miracles.[1] Miracles will make the difference in our century too!"

1.   Ac.2:22

Chapter 11

MAJOR DECISION

I CAN NEVER FORGET how God began to deal with me. As I prayed fervently, He made me to know that if I would make a full consecration to Him, if I would fast and pray and seek His face, that I would share the same power and anointing and ministry as my husband whom I loved and cherished and wanted to be with.

I faced my choices: I could exercise faith and act on God's word, I could preach and teach the gospel, I could cast out devils, I could have power and authority over sicknesses and over demons; or I could remain at home, lead a quiet life and be a happy Christian mother.

The Lord let me know that if I wanted to share in gospel ministry to the world, then it would be my own choice. I was assured that the anointing and power of the Holy Spirit would confirm my ministry.

I knew that to remain at home with our two children, while my husband followed the Lord around the world, would mean that I would have a comfortable home, our children would have a quiet lifestyle with friends, toys, pleasures and a good church influence.

I knew that my needs would be supplied, because my husband was a provider and a lover of his family. Besides, I knew God would never forsake me.

To share in gospel ministry to the world would mean the discomforts of hotels and of crowded quarters for our home, no traditional life for our children, the constant burden of publicity, and the countless other inconveniences of public life which those secluded in private homes can never imagine.

I had always considered my husband's leadings and decisions as directions for us both. But in this particular circumstance, God was giving me a choice which involved a consecration of my own life to His service. It was a decision that only I could make.

A Lifetime Decision

With all of my heart I sought the Lord. I was so thankful that God was giving me this choice.

I made my decision, once and for all. I said, "Yes, Lord, I will be your servant. I will follow You, together with my husband. I want to go all the way. I want Your anointing. I want Your power to work through me. I want to study Your word. I want to be Your representative and messenger, and to teach and to proclaim Your word everywhere."

Within a few weeks our beautiful furniture was sold; everything we had, except a few suit-cases of clothing, was disposed of, and we started out in the ministry of faith, like Abraham and Sarah, not knowing where God would lead us, but we were full of joy and confident that the Lord was with us.

For over five years we never had a bed to call our own. Our babies knew nothing of the freedom that most children enjoy; no fine toys; no nice yards; almost nothing to call their own. Different beds, changing climates, strange food and generally no milk. But they were always healthy, happy and contented. They were blessed in so many ways.

From those days of reconsecration until now, my husband and I have walked together, prayed, fasted and read together, taught and preached together, enjoying the supreme privilege of leading broken, bleeding and suffering humanity to the feet of Jesus where His healing balm soothes and cures every wound.

I would not trade those suitcases today for the loveliest house in the world. I chose to follow my Lord and to share His ministry. That choice holds good today!

Whether preaching in Australia (above), USA (center) or in Africa, Daisy's message is the same: "The gospel message of salvation is for every human person, on the same redemptive basis, regardless of race, culture, color, economic status or gender. It is for whosoever."

Chapter 12

TRIUMPHANT DECADES

I AM INCLUDING one more chapter in Part III (My Positive Choice) as a testimony that *The Woman Believer* can only be limited or restricted in her life and ministry if she chooses restraints.

I never dreamed that my life as a woman, could ever realize such far-reaching dimensions. The details of this chapter are part of my witness that a woman's achievement in ministry depends upon her choice power. I include this information to encourage you to believe that *all things are possible*[1] to *The Woman Believer*.

Four Decades of Fulfillment

For over four decades I have shared triumph after triumph with my husband in our team-ministry of mass evangelism around the world. Our crusades leave an incalculable impact upon nations. That impact is very far-reaching. God has given us favor with statesmen and royalty alike.

In addition to our own mass campaigns, for years we averaged publishing over a ton of gospel literature per day in over 130 languages and dialects. Copies of our documentary crusade films, (and now videos) in over 60 languages, are being used as soulwinning tools to reach multitudes around the world.

Our special crusade sermon cassettes, with battery-operated cassette-players, are teaching millions whom we could never reach personally.

Our books in scores of languages are leading thousands to Christ, as well as being used to train and to encourage pastors, evangelists and lay preachers all over the world.

We are totally involved in soul-saving activities worldwide.

It is a thrill for me to be an integral part of every program we launch for evangelism. My husband and I work together in everything. We plan together, dream together, and minister together. And together, we enjoy the fruits of our labors.

Perhaps one of the greatest visions God ever gave us was that of sponsoring trained national preachers — both women and men, as missionaries to the unreached peoples of their own nations.

That program has set a new pace and has opened broad new horizons in world missions. Today many church organizations have similar programs which were inspired by our pace-setting concept.

While we are engaged in our own mass evangelism crusades and national training conferences around the world, we have successfully directed and nourished a world-wide, full-scale national missionary program in over 100 nations. God has helped us to assist an average of as many as 2,000 national missionaries each month in previously unchurched areas of the world.

Over thirty-thousand trained and qualified national missionaries have already been assisted to minister the gospel to their own unreached people.

An average of 400 new churches have been built and have become self-supporting in a single year. These national pioneer gospel messengers have been supervised by missionaries and national officials of over two hundred different denominations and national church organizations.

It has been amazing to see people from all walks of life taking part in this international missionary program.

The head of a large business in New York City, a publisher in Great Britain, a nurse in New Jersey, a dentist in Oklahoma, a rancher in Australia, a machine operator in Germany, a watchmaker in Switzerland, a farmer in Texas, a lumberman in Canada, a vineyard owner in France, a sacrificing mother on the West Coast — so reads the list of friends and partners who have shared in these tremendous soulwinning outreaches.

Teamwork

To help reduce camera operator costs during our world evangelism journeys, I learned some of the art of photography, which has resulted in ten powerful documentary missionary films.

The first, *Java Harvest* tells how our crusade brought a national gospel awakening to teeming Indonesia.

Among my "credits" is the dramatic feature-length, sound-color film, *Black Gold,* which documents our enormous crusades in Nigeria where tens of thousands turned to Christ and scores of new Christian ministries were birthed.

The film, *Holland Wonder,* records daily crowds of over 100,000 responsive Hollanders during our national crusade there. It is startling proof that gospel ministry is as effective among Europeans as it is on any other continent, when it is confirmed by miracles as in Bible days.

Our lifetime custom has been to start each day with Bible reading and prayer. Together we pray for the needs and special requests of friends and partners with us in evangelism. God answers those prayers with so many wonderful blessings in people's lives.

While we devote ourselves to our preaching, teaching, writing and recording ministries, my responsibilities include administering the vast worldwide soulwinning outreaches of our global network of evangelism.

In addition to this, as the legal Chairperson of this international church organization, my office bears the responsibility of our headquarters and staff, plus our overseas offices and operations in Canada, England, New Zealand and Australia.

In addition to these responsibilities, T.L. depends on me to direct all of our crusades. I may leave at any moment to organize a crusade in some far-flung part of the globe, usually giving four to six weeks to minister in the national churches, plus handling business matters, dealing with the government, organizing the pastors and overseeing the publicity for the crusade.

Then, when the crusade begins, I share in the teaching, preaching, and praying for the multitudes who throng these enormous gospel meetings.

In addition, God still lets me enjoy the pleasure of being a friend, companion and confidante of our children, grandchildren and great-grandchildren!

Over four decades ago when I faced that critical moment of destiny, I did not know what the future held. I only knew that I would share my life with my husband and that I would consecrate my ALL to God's royal service and to His ministry to hurting people worldwide.

I am a witness that God places no restrains upon *The Woman Believer* who uses her choice power to allow Jesus Christ to have unrestricted freedom of ministry to people through her life.

I am truly a fulfilled woman. Thank God, I made the right choice. If it were required of me again, I would say to my husband what Ruth, in the Bible, said to her mother-in-law:

Entreat me not to leave you, or to turn back from following after you; for wherever you go, I will go; and wherever you lodge, I will lodge; your people will be my people, and your God, my God. Where you die, I will die, and there will I be buried.[2]

1.   Mk.9:23
2.   Ru.1:16,17

Life on the road, for Daisy and T.L., makes intimate moments rare, but treasured. Believing their bodies are temples of God, disciplined eating and exercise are part of their lifestyle.

PART IV

THE
DIVINE
SPARK

I HAVE HAD the joy of helping scores of thousands of women around the world to learn how God values them, how He believes in them, and how He trusts them as His *bona fide* representatives.

Every time I see women receiving miracles; when I see their unhappy lives changed, or their defeated, poverty-stricken families discover God's abundant living and prosperity; when I see them discover their restoration to God and become strong witnesses, preachers and leaders in God's work, I see again how much God values women and what can happen through them when His divine spark is ignited in their lives.

Christ's redemptive work is never qualified sexually, any more than it is qualified racially, socially or economically.

This section of *The Woman Believer* will mark a new beginning in your life as a child in God's royal family. You have all of the legal and equal rights to your full family inheritance today. Learn about them and allow the divine spark to be ignited in you.

Chapter 13

THE COST OF NEGATING GOD'S WORD

NOTHING IS MORE vital to a woman's energy and enthusiasm for life than for her to discover and to accept her own value as a God-person, with divine dignity and destiny in His plan.[1]

He created woman as well as man to help Him to develop this planet and to rule this world.[2]

Man and woman sinned against God in the beginning, and allowed Satan to disrupt their state of fellowship and communion, of health and happiness, of blessing and abundance with God.

They were then subject to a new master, Satan. They believed his lie that God did not mean what He said. Then followed the terrible consequences of sin — consequences which are the opposite of what God wants for us:

Instead of forgiveness, there is hatred, malice, suspicion and judgment.

Instead of peace with God, there is unrest and guilt, inferiority and condemnation.

Instead of the Lord's guidance and direction, there is confusion, deceit and perplexity.

Instead of health and energy, there is disease,

sickness and physical suffering.

Instead of abundance, there is poverty, destitution and indigence.

Instead of God's presence, there is loneliness and separation from Him.

Instead of achievement, there is defeat, bondage, repression and enslavement.

But *God so loved the world that He gave His only Son, that whoever believes in Him should not perish but have everlasting life.*[3]

Jesus said, *The thief (Satan) does not come except to steal, and to kill, and to destroy. I have come that they may have life, and that they may have it more abundantly.*[4] The Amplified Version of the Bible says: *that they may have and enjoy life, and have it in abundance to the full, till it overflows.*

1.	Lu.12:6-7	3.	Jn. 3:16
	Ps.8:4-6	4.	Jn.10:10
2.	Ge.1:27-28		
	He.2:6-8		

Chapter 14

WOMEN AND CHRIST'S VICTORY

ABUNDANT LIVING is the life every woman was created for. Here are seven truths of redemption for women who choose life on a full scale.

I.

No woman needs to live under the sentence of death for her sins.[1]

THE LORD IS YOUR RIGHTEOUSNESS.[2]

God has credited the righteousness of His Son to the account of every woman, and you can now have His life and His nature[3] if you believe that Jesus died on the cross to pay the full penalty for all of your sins.[4]

II.

No woman needs to be guilty or to be tormented by her transgressions,[5] or to fear God's judgment.[6]

THE LORD IS YOUR PEACE.[7]

Jesus Christ bore the judgment and suffered the punishment for all of the sins of every woman.[8] Since your penalty never needs to be paid again you can be free and saved. You can have peace. All you need to do is to believe on the Lord Jesus Christ.[9]

III.

No woman needs to be deceived and perplexed, confused and misguided.

THE LORD IS YOUR SHEPHERD.[10]

The Lord wills to be the friend, the partner and the co-worker of every woman. He is your unfailing guide, your director. When you follow Him you will be on the right road.[11] The Good Shepherd gave His life for the sheep, to show you the way.[12] Now you can look to Him and hear His voice and follow Him in the way of true life and health, achievement and abundance.[13]

IV.

No woman needs to be menaced by diseases and infirmities or to be vulnerable to physical weaknesses, suffering and pain.[14]

THE LORD IS YOUR PHYSICIAN.[15]

In His death on the cross, Jesus Christ bore the sicknesses, suffered the pains and carried the infirmities of every woman. Since they were yours, and He did it in your place, *by His sufferings, you are healed*.[16]

V.

No woman needs to be the slave of poverty, of lack or of material deprivation.

THE LORD IS YOUR SOURCE.[17]

Christ put aside all of His riches and became poor on behalf of every woman, so that He might redeem you from want and impart to you His riches.[18]   Now you can share His unlimited supply.[19]   You can enjoy His abundance.   He created all the wealth of this planet and placed it here for the prosperity of every woman, as well as for every man.

Now He wants to enter your life and to share with you His abundant living.

VI.

No woman needs to walk life's road alone; she is no longer forsaken.[20]

THE LORD IS EVER PRESENT.[21]

Jesus Christ wants to be with you always, as your friend and partner — to live His life in you.[22] He died to put away the sins of every woman so that He could commune with you and walk with you again, throughout this life.[23]

Welcome Him into your life and ask Him to make His abode with you.[24]   He will always be with you.[25]

VII.

No woman needs to be enslaved by defeat or by failure, to be held captive by evil or to be dominated by Satan.[26]

THE LORD IS YOUR VICTORY.[27]

Jesus Christ died *to destroy the works of the devil,*[28] then arose from the dead and said: *All authority has been given to Me in heaven and on earth. Lo, I am with you always.*[29]

* * *

That is salvation! That is what it means for a woman to be saved. That is what God wants you as a woman, to enjoy from this very day. He is your eternal source in every aspect of life.

That is not religion. That is life according to God's will for you as a woman — a daughter of God. That is *The Woman Believer* alive today, living in the victory of Christ with the divine spark of real life.

1. Ro.6:23
   Eze.18:4,20
2. Je.23:6;33:16
3. 2Co.5:21
4. 1Pe.2:24
5. Is.1:18
   Col.1:13-14
6. 2Co.5:10
   Ro.5:18
   1Jn.4:17
7. Jud.6:23-24
   Jn.14:27
   Is.53:5
   Col.1:20
8. Is.53:4-5,8,10-12
9. Mk.5:36
10. Ps.23:1
    Jn.10:14
11. Jn.8:12
    Jn.14:6
12. Jn.10:11
    Jn.15:13
13. Jn.10:27-28
14. Is.53:4-5
    Mt.8:17
15. Ex.15:26
16. 1Pe.2:24
17. Ge.22:14
18. 2Co.8:9
19. Jn.10:10
20. Is.41:10
21. Eze.48:35
22. Pr.18:24
    Col.1:27
23. 1Jn.1:3
24. 1Jn.2:24:25
25. Mt.28:20
26. Col.1:13
    1Jn.5:18
27. Ex.17:15
28. 1Jn.3:8
29. Mt.28:18,20

Chapter 15

NEW LIFESTYLE FOR THE WOMAN BELIEVER

YOUR SEVEN FOLD NEEDS have now been met by His seven fold abundance. Today marks a new beginning in your life as a daughter in God's royal family.

God has opened the way for you as a woman, to be healthy, successful, happy and productive.

You ask: Is it difficult?

In one sense, yes! Because, as a woman, your thinking process will probably need to be adjusted. You will need to fill new creative roles in life, to accept new ideas and to learn to talk and to act differently. And this can be tough if you object to change.

Once you have allowed your lifestyle to be cemented in a subservient role, and once you have fixed the blame for your problems on others, it will be extremely difficult for you to adjust. The toughest barrier that obstructs a woman from changing is often herself. Her own thoughts and words and deeds are the seeds that create the environment, the problems, the frustrations and many of the illnesses that plague her.[1]

The greatest insurance on earth for a woman's success in life is to personally identify with God.

You simply cannot fail when you recognize Him as your partner.[2]

Around the world women are searching for purpose, for identity, for freedom of action and of expression — for God's divine spark in their lives. They want to know the reality of God. They want to know that the Bible is true — and if so, how to make a practical application of it in their own lives.

Religion has failed to communicate to women their divine value to God as His representatives and co-workers.

1.   Pr.6:2   2.   Is.41:10
      Pr.21:23   Is.54:17
      Ps.141:3   Is.55:10-11
      Ja.1:26
      1 Pe.3:10
      Col.4:6
      Pr.15:23
      2Ti.1:7
      2Co.10:5
      Ph.4:8
      Is.26:3

Chapter 16

EQUALITY IN GOD'S PLAN

CAN WHAT THE Bible calls salvation be a real, practical experience for a woman the same as for a man? Can she truly be re-born? If so, is she redeemed from her past the same as a man is?

Is the original sin of a woman still held against her, while the original sin of a man is forgiven and forgotten?

The business world recognizes the equality of women and is solving the problems of traditional sexual inequities. But in the church, if a woman discovers her equality in God's plan of redemption and if she talks about it or acts on her discovery, she is usually ignored or reprimanded as being insubordinate and out of order.

Because of the sexual bias fostered by traditional ecclesiasticism, millions of women have abandoned their faith altogether, concluding that clerical canons and dogmas are too inflexible to ever permit them to fully function as Christ's representatives.

No Longer Second Class

I have been privileged to proclaim the good news to literally millions of people, face to face. Tens of thousands of women have been enriched by simple faith in God and I have watched them reap their rich harvest in many nations of the world.

But ecclesiastical orthodoxy has hindered God's redemptive plan for millions of women in this century.

Archaic censorship and discrimination of Christian women in our modern world becomes a demoralizing influence that smothers their imagination and their creativity in God's work.

Instead of the divine spark being ignited in women, their inspiration and enthusiasm are often stifled.

Outdated religious canons and the misrepresentation of scriptural passages concerning women have resulted in the church of Jesus Christ being the only remaining public institution in which women are generally adjudged inferior, repressed and subordinated, forbidden from public initiative, and restrained from leadership.

Parochial discrimination against womankind repudiates Paul's revelation and teaching of redemption, of reconciliation, of justification and of restoration to God for every human person, whether male or female.

Hope for Women in the Church?

This indignifying deprecation of women which relegates them to the inveterate status of inferiority, explains why so many educated young women have despaired of hope for achievement within church ranks, and have pursued other options.

A young Parisian collegiate asked: "Who needs a God in our industrialized world of science?

What intelligent woman would submit herself to outdated religious dictums which reduce her to a second class status?"

A young Brussels philosophy major ridiculed faith in God as she reasoned: "We enjoy the greatest psychological discoveries ever known. The ills of society can better be cured through the miracles of psychoanalysis, than through bigoted religion with its medieval discrimination against women."

Whether one-by-one, group-by-group, or nation-by-nation, the multi-national gospel ministry of Daisy inspires women, as well as men, to discover true dignity, peace and happiness in the non-judgmental role of Christ's love-representatives in life. Here she shares with university students on the steps of the Buddhist Marble Temple in Bangkok.

Chapter 17

LET THE LIGHT TURN ON

AROUND THE WORLD, whether on the busy streets of Paris, New York or Bogota; whether in village towns of the Philippines, India, China or Africa, I see women's instinctive search for a living God — for the divine spark of inspiration for meaningful living.

For women to know that God is interested in them as His friends and partners contradicts most of what they have learned from religion and culture.

I have watched the light turn on in the faces of tens of thousands of women when they realized that God loves them and that He paid the same price to redeem them as He paid for men.

Capable and talented women can no longer allow their voices to be stifled, their influence to be limited, and their lives to be deprecated through the bias fostered by religion and culture.

Millions of women own nothing, yet they live in a world of abundance. Why? It is usually because they have submitted to a role of subservience, rather than assuming responsibility for their own lives by putting their God-given talents and abilities to work for the good of their world. They have lacked the divine spark of inspiration that comes by understanding God's redemptive plan for women and how He values them the same as He values men.

Women whose bodies should be vibrant and
healthy in service to God and to others, allow
themselves to deteriorate physically. Why? Because the traditional role in which religion and culture casts them, stifles creativity and represses
initiative toward achievement in life.

It is time for the divine spark of inspiration to
be ignited in the life of *The Woman Believer*.

Chapter 18

FANTASTIC FACTS

THE ANSWER TO the male/female disparities in culture and in religion lies in understanding: 1) God's original plan for humanity, and 2) how Christ died to redeem every person to God — women the same as men, and to restore them to His side, as partners and friends, as though no sin had ever been committed.

Here are 16 facts for *The Woman Believer:*

FACT 1: Christ's redemption is the same for a woman as it is for a man.

FACT 2: A woman is reconciled to God and is justified from all past sin the same as a man is.

FACT 3: The promises of our Lord are for women exactly as they are for men.

FACT 4: When a woman believes on Christ, she is accepted as His follower and as His representative the same as a man who believes on Him.

FACT 5: A woman who believes on Christ is authorized to do the works of Christ the same as a man is.

FACT 6: The commission of Christ applies to women believers the same as it does to men believers.

FACT 7: *These signs shall follow* women who believe the same as they shall follow men who believe.

FACT 8: Women believers are authorized to heal the sick, to cast out devils, to cleanse the lepers, to raise the dead, to preach the gospel, the same as men are.

FACT 9: The anointing and the power of the Holy Spirit has the same purpose in a woman's life as it has in a man's life.

FACT 10: The gifts of the Holy Spirit are bestowed upon and function through women believers exactly the same as through men believers.

FACT 11: Jesus Christ has promised to be with a woman believer, to confirm the gospel she propagates, the same as He is with a man believer.

FACT 12: Women believers constitute the body of Christ in the same sense that men believers do.

FACT 13: All of the ministries and offices which God has set in the church of Jesus Christ function through women the same as through men who make up His body.

FACT 14: The church of Jesus Christ is made up of women believers the same as of men believers.

FACT 15: The Bible is for women and men believers alike.

FACT 16: God's covenants, His promises, His

testaments, His agreements are for women the same as they are for men.

Salvation is not sexual any more than it is racial.

The church of Jesus Christ is no more qualified sexually than it is racially.

The promulgation of God's love plan by the church can never be qualified racially, sexually, economically, or socially.

Women are affected by the gospel, and are to be involved in its propagation, in its establishment, in its disciplines, and in its accomplishments in the same way that men are.

We are no longer Jews or Greeks or slaves or free people or even men or women, but we are all the same — we are Christians; we are one in Jesus Christ.[1]

Those facts ignite the divine spark in women, and those facts become the vital source of inspiration in life. They open the wide doors of freedom which lead to a fresh new abundant lifestyle of service to God and to people.

Spiritually, God wills that every woman have peace, tranquility, faith, love, creativity and abundant living.

Physically, God offers to women healing, energy, a strong body, robust health.

Materially, God offers to women success,

achievement, prosperity, and access to the divine source of all of His provisions.

Through Christ's death on behalf of humanity, He opened the way for every woman and every man to come to Him, and for Him to come to you.

Christ's Power in You

Traditional religion has handed down a limited concept of God's relationship with women believers.

Spirituality for a woman is considered to be a submissive demeanor of self-resignation to a state of material poverty, of non-assertive subordination, of non-creativity and of general female subservience.

Women are learning to extricate themselves from that inferiority syndrome, as they discover the truths of God's non-sexual redemptive plan.

In order to accomplish good things for yourself, for others and for God, discover that God is at work in you. Discover the purpose God has for you, as well as your true value and recognize the innate abilities, the power, the anointing and the promises of God which are yours.

God is alive in you as a woman. See yourself as God sees you. Discover your female roots in royalty. Think of yourself as God thinks of you. Talk of yourself as He does — in the Bible.

That will ignite the divine spark — the miraculous positive drive of Christ's power inside of you. As His seeds of truth and faith are planted in you, they produce God's kind of woman — *The Woman Believer*.

When your mind perceives God's abundance and begins to comprehend that He created the wealth of this earth for the blessing of women the same as for men, the walls of mental enslavement will crumble and the rainbow of your own dignity and destiny in God's redemptive plan will come into clear focus.

Redemptive Inheritance

When Moses decided to possess the rich land which God had prepared for His people, he sent twelve spies to investigate. Numbers, Chapters 13-14.

The overwhelming majority took one look at that wealthy land, and fled. They said, "It's too good to be true. This land of milk and honey cannot be for us. Giants are there. We felt like grasshoppers. They can destroy us" See Nu.13:27-33.

They thought that way. They talked that way. They acted that way. Consequently, they reaped that crop. They never inherited the abundance which God wanted them to possess. They died without ever entering the domain God had planned for them.

That is what religious indoctrination has caused millions of women to do ever since Christ came and redeemed them. They have said: "This is too good to be true. Women cannot rise to this level. This land belongs to the men!" And millions of

women have died without pride and without fulfillment, never having experienced the blessings and the
achievements provided for them in redemption.

Only two of Moses' committee looked at things
like God saw them, and spoke like God. They
said in essence: "This is a good land and since we
are God's people, He must have created it for us
to enjoy. We shall possess it." And they inherited
it!

Thousands of God's royal daughters, around the
world, are reappraising theological pronouncements
about women, and are moving into their redemptive
inheritance in God's work today.

That inheritance is available to every woman
who has the courage to believe in her restoration to
God, and who has enough self-value to walk out of
the female chamber where theology has kept her
quarantined in self-effacing submission, to fulfill
her God-ordained role as a fully qualified partner
in His redemptive plan for humanity.

1.   Ga.3:28 LB

Chapter 19

OPEN DOOR TO GOD'S BEST

WHEN ANY WOMAN receives Jesus Christ, she is infused with new energy. She simply cannot be defeated, and she is not alone anymore. She has discovered the power of His presence in her life — the divine spark.

The gates of hell cannot prevail against a woman when God is on her side.

Open the doors of your mind to God's way of thinking. Disease and pain are not part of God's plan for women. Poverty and lack in a woman's life do not bring glory to Him who is the source of all abundance. Inferiority and second class person-hood do not belong to the daughters of God's royal family.

Accept yourself as God's kind of being, without limitations and without restrictions.

Walk out of mental insignificance like so many other women are doing, and move up with God into His royal family personhood, with all of the legal and the equal rights of every member of His household.

The devil never wanted you to discover your identity, equality, divine dignity or your destiny as a woman in God's redemptive plan. But God is coming to you through this book to confirm His love for you and to reveal His plan for your life.

Happiness, success, health and abundance will start growing up all around you. The divine spark has been ignited in you.

Seeds of God's Blessings

The Bible says: *These blessings shall come upon you and OVERTAKE you, if you obey the voice of the Lord.*[1]

If you are traveling forty miles per hour, God's *blessings* will travel fifty miles per hour to *overtake* you.

You are a seed planter whether you realize it or not. The situation around you is the harvest of the seeds you have planted or that you have allowed to be planted in your life.

Wise and successful people have all learned, sooner or later, that any desired change of their environment must begin inside themselves.

You grow your own circumstances by the thoughts and words and deeds which you sow every day. They are the seeds you plant.

Since thoughts always come first, all changes begin in you — not in others.

Do not make the mistake of trying to change others. Do not even try to change yourself. Just feed into yourself the right information, and you will automatically become what you plant in yourself.

By reading this book, seeds of truth are being sown in your life which will produce inevitable harvests of improved self-image, of raised aspirations, of deepened confidence and of new courage to pursue new dreams and to achieve new conquests in life.

The Bible says to you: *My child, give attention to My words; incline your ear to My sayings. Do not let them depart from your eyes; keep them in the midst of your heart.*[2]

The poorest woman on earth has a right to plant the seeds of God's blessings and to reap their harvest in her own life.

How God Values Women

I have had the joy of helping scores of thousands of women around the world to learn that God values them, that He believes in them, that He trusts them as His *bona fide* representatives.

Every time I see women receiving miracles; when I see their unhappy lives changed, or their defeated, poverty-stricken families discover God's abundant living and prosperity; when I see them discover their restoration to God and become strong witnesses, preachers and leaders in God's work, I see again how much God values women and what can happen through them when His divine spark is ignited in their lives.

We have been reliving the gospels and the book of Acts for over four decades.

As we open our mail and read the testimonies of changed lives that come to us from all over the world, I get so happy that I want to share with every woman in the whole world the good news of Jesus Christ.

So many women write to me about their problems and hurts, about their struggles and sicknesses, about their depressions and emptiness.

I just want to tell them about the books and the inspiring audio and video cassettes which my husband, T.L. Osborn and I have prepared. They are packed with the divine seeds of truth which, when planted in a woman's life, will lift her from insignificance to self-esteem, from resignation to achievement, from unhappiness to fulfillment, from sickness and infirmity to health, from poverty to self-sufficiency, from mediocrity to excellence.

So often, people who are enslaved by circumstances or by some person, have allowed themselves to get into these situations through their own mistakes or lack of self-value and of self-direction. This can all be changed by planting the right seeds.

1.   De.28:2 RSV
2.   Pr.4:20-21

Chapter 20

POWER TO CHANGE THINGS

THERE IS NO reason for *The Woman Believer* to live in pessimism, reacting to those who demean her; she cannot submit to restrictive ecclesiastical doctrines, or to cultural restraints, when God has given her the power and the anointing of His Spirit in order to change her world.

I.

INSTEAD OF BEING angry and instead of blaming religious or cultural inequities, *The Woman Believer* can discover that God made this world, with all of its material and spiritual blessings for her, and that He redeemed her and sent His Holy Spirit upon her to act as His representative in bringing blessing to the hurting people of her own world.

II.

INSTEAD OF LIVING under the fear of being condemned, of being misjudged or of being disliked, *The Woman Believer* can discover that God's plan has transferred to her account the righteousness and the dignity of Jesus Christ, and recognize that it is He who lives in her as a woman, and who ministers through her — that He is the same in and through her as He is in and through any man.

III.

INSTEAD OF LIVING in torment with oneself, out of harmony with family and friends; instead of transferring those mental anguishes to one's own body, or business, or environment, ruining one's own health and happiness by their poison, *The Woman Believer* can discover how God has a miracle plan for her as a woman, how He can change her in one moment, and how He can transfer His life, His power and His anointing to her and make her a success as His representative and agent to needy people in her own world.

IV.

INSTEAD OF GOING on in confusion, making wrong decisions, stumbling into failure and every conceivable trap of defeat, *The Woman Believer* can discover that God believes in her as a woman, and that He trusts her as His representative.

Resolve to arise and to experience the success, the health, the prosperity and the fulfillment that He wills for you to enjoy as a woman in His service.

Then go out and bless your world by sharing God's goodness with people. Whatever dream He plants in your heart, cooperate with Him and bring that dream to fruition. He is the source of all of the energy, the ability, the talent and the money needed to see your dream blossom and prosper.

V.

INSTEAD OF SUBJECTING oneself to disease and sickness, living vulnerable to every physical plague that ravages human beings, *The Woman Believer* can discover God's abundant miracle power to heal her as a woman, not only of diseases, inferiorities and inadequacies, but also to keep her and her house in health, happiness and success.

VI.

INSTEAD OF BELIEVING in poverty and want; instead of being a victim of circumstances and instead of living one's life on a hand-to-mouth existence, *The Woman Believer* can discover that God created all the wealth of this world and that He placed it here for her blessing and for her prosperity. As a woman, count on Him as your partner in life.

VII.

INSTEAD OF LONELINESS and fear, discouragement and depression, *The Woman Believer* can discover that God wants to become her partner and co-worker; that He wants to make His abode at her house so that she can know the joy of success, happiness, achievement, health and prosperity.

VIII.

INSTEAD OF TRYING and failing in life, instead of never bringing home the victory and of never knowing success, *The Woman Believer* can make the glorious discovery that God is a winner and that when He is on her team, she as a woman

always wins the prize. Learn to live the good life*
with the God of abundance and success as your
confidant and partner.

Think as big and as good as God is big and
good.

Think health, achievement, success, love and
abundant living, because this is God's will for
every child in His royal family.

His divine spark is ignited in you when you
align yourself with His word and become *The
Woman Believer* He designed you to be.

---

* Be sure to get my husband's remarkable 304 page book, *The
Good Life*, originally written for new believers throughout
the French speaking world, and later published in English.

PART V

MATERIAL BLESSINGS FOR
WOMEN

WHEN GOD FORMED Eve, He placed her, with her man, in the beautiful garden of abundant living. There was total prosperity for Eve, the same as for Adam. It was what God designed every woman to live in.

It is not logical for a woman's academic and business potential to be wasted in the monotonous, non-creative world of pushbuttons and soap operas.

To restrict *The Woman Believer* today to a role which befit her foremothers, would be like limiting men to the mechanisms of the horse-and-buggy era because they befit the image of their forefathers.

The world of abundance that God has created all around you is proof that He wills prosperity for women the same as He does for men.

Decide that God is depending on you, as a woman, to accomplish His work. There is nothing impossible for God and you.

Chapter 21

THE JESUS WOMAN IN TODAY'S WORLD

DOES GOD WILL material prosperity for *The Woman Believer?* Or is it God's plan for the daughters of His family to be dependent upon men for their material needs in order to keep them humble, submissive and subservient?

The fact is that the Bible abounds with clearcut promises of prosperity and of material abundance for both women and men, when they regard money positively — as a means for accomplishing God's purpose on earth.

Biblical promises are for *The Woman Believer* who identifies with Christ the same as they are for the man believer.

Women and Productivity

There is a traditional concept, particularly in religions and cultures handed down from earlier societies that God never endowed women with the intellectual capacity for achievement in business or with the faculties for success in enterprise.

It is a paradox to this notion, that throughout most of the non-industrialized world, women are often the real entrepreneurs, respected for their innate business and marketing ingenuity.

This concept also contradicts the Biblical characteristics of the Proverbs woman who not only is an efficient homemaker, faithful wife and intelligent mother, but she is competent in real estate dealings, enterprise, personnel management, productive and quality manufacturing, financial administration, public marketing, family responsibility, successful industry, education, societal influence, leadership, material prosperity, generosity, philanthropy, positive human relationships, dignity and self-esteem, public prestige, recognition, attractiveness, honor, community distinction, entrepreneurial initiative, educational skill, psychological wisdom, prudence, and in general, she is the epitome of a capable, happy, esteemed, successful, influential and prosperous woman.[1]

Yet, in the modernized world, religion and culture combine to foster an anomalous and irrational ideal for women.

Although women are expected to be educated and academically competent, as soon as they are married, it is assumed that they will accept passively their assigned roles in life and graciously adapt to subordinate, submissive and subservient functions in society. What a contrast to the Proverbs woman.

In today's modern society, after a woman accepts a man in her life, it is often presumed that she will affably relinquish whatever career, vocation or profession she had aspired to or was involved in, abdicating her scholastic qualifications in favor of becoming a good and proper wife. Often, this means being a general unpaid maid and servant to the man she has married. This attitude does not create the atmosphere needed for a Biblical relationship in marriage, nor does it express the successful woman of Bible times.

Because of this traditional propensity, millions of Christian women today fail to develop their innate talents and abilities, living out their lives in resigned subordination, usually without ever entertaining the idea of material accomplishment or of creative productivity such as expressed by the lifestyle of the Proverbs woman.

Time and Energy Savers

I was born and raised in Merced, California, one of eleven children. We eked out a meager subsistence, farming the ground and working in the orchards.

Being the tenth child, I remember watching my mother toil day and night as the homemaker.

All the water for household needs had to be pumped from the well. Then it was carried in buckets to our rough, wood-floor kitchen. Mama built and stoked the fire to heat it in a big iron kettle for washing. She spent hours of backbreaking drudgery over the galvanized washtub and scrub board, toiling to keep the family's homemade clothes and threadbare bedding clean.

Mama sewed all of our clothes, hand-knitted all of our sweaters, socks and woolens; grew the vegetables, cooked every meal over a wood stove, churned the butter, scrubbed the floors on her hands and knees, canned the fruit, hand-quilted our bedding, baked our bread, *etc.*

That is a *bona fide* "homemaker." The lack of labor-saving machines made the task of home-making a full time job. No wonder the family's survival depended on her expertise.

But by what twist of human logic does religion and culture insist that the modern wife, with a hi-tech equipped house, conform to the image of my mama?

Today's modern housewife and househusband have the advantages of quick-pack, well balanced, frozen dinners and microwave ovens, sealed or canned foods, bottled drinks and quick-serve desserts; pushbutton dishwashers, garbage disposals, washers, dryers, vacuum cleaners, running hot and cold water, paper dishes, plastic dinnerware, disposable diapers, ready-made clothing, electric blankets, and so much more — all valued time and energy savers.

Forefathers and Foremothers

To restrict *The Woman Believer* today to a role which befit her foremothers, would be like the religious dictums which limit men to the mechanisms of the horse-and-buggy era because they befit the image of their forefathers.

Maintaining Creativity

This outdated ideal for a woman gradually stifles her creativity as she surrenders to the self-image of perennial servitude and of dependent submission. Such a surrender neutralizes much of her inherent skill and resourcefulness.

By the time the children of a contemporary woman are in school, if she has not chosen to, or been allowed to exercise her innate or acquired expertise and her skill potential, she may unwittingly lose her drive for accomplishment, and actually come to prefer the comforts of her traditional dependency.

When that happens, something precious and vital dies in the woman. The man in her life has usually done the pivotal thinking and has made the principal decisions concerning her life. The creative strategy for survival or for growth has never been cultivated by her. It has been considered the prerogative of her husband to do such thinking. Consequently the woman has likely never sensed the satisfaction of material productivity nor the self-esteem of entrepreneurial achievement.

Often, women who are divorced or widowed, find themselves unexercised in strategic planning or in enterprise, incompetent in business or marketing, inexperienced in the workplace, unqualified for employment and unaccustomed to the simplest professional requirements for life.

Many women have never experienced the common dignity of having a personal bank account, of owning a piece of property or even an automobile in their own name, or of signing a business contract. Many of them have never written a check or have never made the most ordinary business decision or transaction.

When we elevate the status of women, we elevate the world. The example of the Proverbs

woman can help to motivate a re-awakening of this
unlimited potential in *The Woman Believer* when, by
knowledge, she transcends the demeaning indignities
and inequities of quaint traditions of the past and
develops new self-esteem through the exercise of
her own talents, through her own initiative and
through the rewards of her own accomplishments in
life.

1.   Pr.31:10-31

Chapter 22

WOMEN PARTNERS WITH GOD

GOD WILLS material blessings for women, but they must apply themselves in creative thinking, in enterprise and in industry in a competitive world, as the Proverbs woman did and as all successful people must do.

I have written this book to encourage you, as a believing woman, to discover your own dignity and your own destiny in God's plan, as His friend and as His partner in representing Him in our world.

Allow your indigenous talents and innate abilities to come to life; not at the expense of your family and marriage, but because of them.

Become alert to your own potential. Reach out and become a learner. Upgrade your own attitude.

Decide that God is depending on you as a woman, to accomplish His work as much as He depends on any man. Believe for Him to impart His wisdom to you. There is nothing impossible for God and *The Woman Believer*.

To experience the material blessings God wills for you, a woman must accept His promises, claim them and ACT on them — exactly like an unsaved person who accepts forgiveness or like a sick person who receives healing by faith.

You will do that when you, as a woman, decide to liberate yourself from the distorted and restricted female image of the past, and apply yourself as a capable, positive, creative producer in your world.

As a woman believer, are you willing to be a finance-partner with God in lifting and in blessing hurting and despairing people?

Is your attitude: "My place, as a woman, is to concede in life and to fill whatever role others expect of me?"

Or is it: "As a woman, I choose to identify with God in His love plan for people. I understand that money can be a sacred tool for soulwinning. I will be God's partner to reach hurting human persons and to bless them as the Proverbs woman did — starting with own my family."

Giving to reach souls, is a ministry in itself. To *The Woman Believer* money represents her life.

When she invests it to reach the unsaved, she is as much a minister or a missionary as the one who goes and announces the good news to the people.

But unless a woman decides to become active in some wage-earning or money-producing enterprise in her own name, like the Proverbs woman did, how can she become an effective finance-partner with God and discover the exhilaration and the self-esteem of accomplishments with Him?

From Abundance to Scarcity

When God created the first woman and man, He placed them in a world of material plenty. He commanded the waters and the ground *to bring forth abundantly.*[1] *God blessed them, saying, Be fruitful, and multiply.*[2] Then he placed Adam and Eve in control of this abundance.

But Satan's intervention in God's love plan enticed the woman and the man to sin against God, which resulted in their separation from Him.[3]

God said to them: *Cursed is the ground for your sake; in sorrow shall you eat of it all the days of your life. Both thorns and thistles it shall bring forth for you, ... in the sweat of your face shall you eat bread, until you return to the ground.*[4]

Now you can understand the reason for human destitution. It was never God's ideal. He planned that women and men be blessed materially.

The economic problems which exasperate and harass women are the issue of the deeper problem of estrangement from God's principles for life.

Every way you turn there are demands placed upon you with which you cannot cope. Food, clothing and shelter — the bare necessities of life are secured only by constant struggle.

In the midst of a world of God's abundance, you toil, you borrow, you mortgage — and in spite of all you can do, there is often not enough to make ends meet at your house. This is the devil's strategy to break your will and to reduce you to the level of slavery.

You Were Not Made to Struggle

God never created women for such a struggle in life. When He created Eve, He placed her, with her man, in the most beautiful garden of abundant living. There was total prosperity for Eve, the same as for Adam. It was what God designed every woman to live in. It was His dream of contentment, of harmony, of abundance.

Then the master deceiver paid them a visit and they yielded to his subtle temptation to question what God had said.[5]

Through their *lust of the flesh* and their *pride of life*,[6] Adam and Eve partook of the forbidden fruit[7] transgressing God's law, thereby forfeiting the garden of blessing which He had given to them.[8]

Greed, jealousy, lust and deceit produced the evils of human society where the strong dominated the weak, where the rich ruled over the poor, where the men subjected the women, where lords became masters over peasants — all of which was the result of sin.

Pleasure gave way to anguish.

Happiness and love turned to discontentment and lust.

Health became poisoned by disease.

Abundance degenerated into want, destitution and depravity.

God's dream for people was aborted.

God Is Spirit!
You Are His Flesh!

Jesus explained it all when He said:

The thief (Satan) *comes only to steal, and to kill, and to destroy.*[9]

But God *is not willing that any should perish, but that all should come to repentance.*[10]

You, as a woman, were not born to be a slave, but to be an *heir of God, a joint-heir with Jesus Christ*[11] — to be God's friend and partner.

You see, God is Spirit. You, as a woman, are His flesh. Whatever He does, He does it through His body — the church, which is people — ordinary women and men like you and me.[12]

1.	Ge.1:20	6.	1Jn.2:16	11.	Ro.8:16-17
2.	Ge.1:22	7.	Ge.3:6,8		Ga.3:29
3.	Is.59:2	8.	Ge.3:23-24	12.	1Co.3:16;6:19;
4.	Ge.3:17-19	9.	Jn.10:10		Ep.2:21-22
5.	Ge.3:1	10.	2Pe.3:9		

Daisy says, "Religion, culture and tradition provide an abundance of excuses which discourage many women from doing what Christ commissioned them to do."

Chapter 23

GOD'S RETURN IS ABUNDANT

GOD'S PRIORITY is to share the gospel with every creature, in all the world.[1]

The highest priority that *The Woman Believer* can have is to be part of God's plan for humanity. To do that, she learns about God's prosperity-plan for herself, and she appropriates His plan for material blessing in her own life so she can share the effects of her prosperity with her world.

When I was just a little girl, I learned from my mother and father how to take tiny seeds and sow them in the rich farm soil. I marveled at how much God gave us in return for the small amount which we gave to the earth.

Jesus taught that every promise He gave was a seed. He said, *The seed is the word of God.*[2] That seed of His promise is *incorruptible*[3] (undecaying, immortal, imperishable). The life in each seed of God's promise cannot die or decay or perish. God's seed promises cannot fail.

Christ said: *The words that I speak to you are spirit, and they are life.*[4]

There is life in each seed. That life is from God — the author of life.

Every time good seed is sown in good soil, the sower reaps an increased return. This law is as irrefutable as the law of gravity.

It is impossible for a woman to plant one kernel of corn and to reap only one kernel in return.

God wants women to see that *it is He who gives you power to get wealth.*[5] *Riches and wealth are the gift of God.*[6]

God wants *The Woman Believer* to realize that giving and receiving money is a flowing interchange between her act of faith and His unlimited supply. It is based on His infallible law of sowing and reaping.

A farmer sets aside the choice grain (the *firstfruits*) and gives it back to the earth. In return, the good soil gives back an abundance of the same kind of seed that was sown, and that farmer's *barns are filled with plenty.*[7] That way, the farmer has more to sow — in greater fields.

Blessed is the woman who fears the Lord, who delights greatly in His commandments. Wealth and riches shall be in her house.[8] *The Lord has pleasure in the prosperity of His* (woman as well as man) *servant.*[9]

See yourself as a woman partner with God — His finance-partner, one into whose care He can entrust His wealth in a flow of giving and receiving. Then expect God's miracle return, *pressed down, shaken together, running over.*[10] He will do it if He must perform a material miracle to do it.

Material Miracles — For Women?

God performed a material miracle to provide money for His disciples to pay their taxes.[11]

God performed a material miracle to provide bread and meat and water for the Israelites in the wilderness.[12] He even miraculously prevented their shoes from wearing out.[13]

God performed a material miracle for a widow whose creditors were coming to take her sons as bond-servants. Miraculously she poured enough oil from a single cruse to fill many vessels full, which she sold for money to pay her creditors. It was a material miracle.[14]

Jesus Christ performed a material miracle to supply food for five thousand hungry people in the desert — women, men and children.[15]

The question is: Will God perform a material miracle to supply your needs?

Will God save an unconverted woman? Yes, if she knows His covenant, believes His promises and acts upon them in faith.

Will God heal a sick woman? Yes, if she knows His covenant of healing, believes His promises and acts upon them in faith.

Will God multiply the finances or miraculously increase the possessions of a woman? Yes, if she knows His covenant of prosperity and acts upon His promises in faith.

The Woman Believer
and God's Promises

Christian women believe that Bible verses promising salvation are for them the same as they are for men. But few of them claim the multitude of Biblical promises in which God assures women, as well as men, of material prosperity.

Women believers do not hesitate to claim: *Whoever shall call on the name of the Lord shall be saved.*[16] *You shall receive power after that the Holy Spirit has come upon you.*[17] *Lo I am with you alway, even to the end of the world.*[18]

But few Christian women claim verses like those included in this book which concern material blessings. As you read them, ask yourself: "Do I truly believe these Bible verses are for me as a woman?" And if you do, claim them and begin to appropriate God's material blessings through positive, active faith.

For example, *The Woman Believer* has the right to read 3 John 2 like this: *Beloved daughter of mine, I wish above all things, that you may prosper and be in health, even as your soul prospers.*[19]

Prosper in that verse means "to succeed, thrive, be successful; to be safe in mind, body and material estate; to have peace and a secure welfare; to be secure and wealthy." That describes God's desire for *The Woman Believer* today.

Theology says, "No! This cannot be!"

If you agree with that negative position, Jesus said, *You make the word of God of none effect by your tradition,* (which is "an inherited culture, attitude or belief.")[20]

These words, *of none effect,* actually mean "to cancel or to void God's promises by contrary beliefs or traditions."

Webster's Dictionary says this means "to reduce to nothing, to make void, to render of no legal value, to destroy the force of."

As a woman, you can "reduce God's word to nothing" or "render it of no legal value" or "destroy its force" or "annul and invalidate it" *by your tradition.*[21]

That is what you do to His promises about prosperity if you embrace the belief that God wants you as a woman, to be subordinated in life without personal means, without material achievements, without the self-pride of personal enterprise and without the self-esteem and the dignity of realizing personal material success.

The traditional belief that material blessing for women is wrong, or that financial achievement is only for men, nullifies God's plan for the prosperity of *The Woman Believer.*

But when you as a woman, read God's promises and act on them, God will fulfill them in your life — even if He must perform material miracles to do it, like miraculously multiplying the widow's oil and meal, or the lad's lunch that fed five thousand people.

1.	Mk.16:15	8.	Ps.112:1,3	15.	Mt.14:14-21
2.	Lu.8:11	9.	Ps.35:27	16.	Ro.10:13
3.	1Pe.1:23	10.	Lu.6:38	17.	Ac.1:8
4.	Jn.6:63	11.	Mt.17:27	18.	Mt.28:20
5.	De.8:18	12.	Ps.78:20,24-29	19.	3Jn.1:2
6.	Ec.5:19	13.	De.29:5	20.	Mt.15:6
7.	Pr.3:9-10	14.	2K.4:1-7	21.	Mt. 15:6

Chapter 24

GOD'S WORD – GOD'S MIRACLES FOR WOMEN

I HAVE RECEIVED so many testimonies from women who have learned to give by faith in God's word, then who have experienced His miraculous return. When they began, they were wage earners. Today they are owners of businesses. When they began, they were renters. Today they are property owners. They put God's word to the test and they experienced His prosperity in return.

The Lord will grant you plenty of goods, in the increase of your livestock, and in the produce of your ground.[1]

Plenty in that verse means "to exceed, to excel, to abound, to profit, to be abundant." It means "yielding abundantly more than sufficient; a great or rich supply; generous sufficiency; large supply; copious yield."

In other words, the Bible says: "The Lord will make you abundant and generous in goods; He will give you a great and rich supply."

These promises are for you as a woman, the same as they are for any man. Claim them in faith. Act upon them and God will materialize them in your life.

Like the Proverbs woman, when you combine the attributes of honesty, of integrity, of industry and of commitment in a lifestyle of positive faith and of diligent endeavor, God's laws of compensation, of sowing and of reaping, guarantee your achievement.

I encourage *The Woman Believer* to take a long, renewed look at these wonderful Biblical statements which I am including, and to embrace their principles in a fresh attitude of personal faith and commitment to their materialization in your own life.

The Lord will command the blessing on you in your storehouses and in all to which you set your hand to do.[2]

Blessed shall be the fruit of your body, and the produce of your ground and the increase of your cattle and the offering of your flocks.[3]

Blessed shall be your basket and your store.[4]

These are promises made to every Jesus-woman, *if you will hearken to the voice of the Lord and observe His commandments.*[5]

God's will is *that you, always having all sufficiency in all things, may have an abundance for every good work.*[6]   God wills that you be *enriched in everything for all liberality.*[7]   He wills your *liberal sharing ... to all people.*[8]   To do this, God wills your prosperity and He has provided abundant promises to back up His will.

It is He who gives you power to get wealth,[9] and it is He who set in order His principle of sowing and reaping for women as well as for men.

It Actually Happened to Us

I remember a time of dire financial need when my husband and I were young. I did not have a coat. It was during a time of rainy, cold weather in California. We were riding public transportation to preach the gospel.

We attended a conference where the urgent need for a large missionary printing press was presented. Before that conference ended, we borrowed a hundred dollars and planted it as seed-money in the Lord's work, to help buy that press. (That was a large gift in those days.)

Very soon we were reaping an abundant return from that seed-gift. A woman bought me a beautiful new coat. A man presented us the title to an automobile. Money came from unexpected sources. God's law did not fail.

Another time, our faith was tested. We had purchased a car and we planned to pay for it through monthly installments. But that particular month we had given everything we had received.

Whenever we saw an opportunity to win more souls, we planted our seed-money. We believed that the more we planted, the larger return we could claim. Our needs were large, so we planted liberally.

Our car payment was due. We lacked fourteen dollars. We had sown our seed-money, so we were believing for God's abundant return.

We prayed earnestly for God to meet our need. We knew the seed-dollars which we had sown must produce an increased return — even if God had to perform a material miracle. We were proving God — putting Him to the test as He said to do.[10]

That night, we locked the door of our small room and went to bed. No one knew our needs but God alone.

What happened that night will sound ridiculous and incredible in the natural, but it is true. God performed a material miracle to prove His promises in our lives.

When we awoke, one-dollar bills were strewn all over that room, as though they had literally been dropped from heaven, fluttering down onto the bed, the floor, behind the table, under the divan, *etc.*

We gathered up the dollar bills as reverently as the children of Israel gathered the manna from heaven,[11] or as the disciples gathered the fragments of bread which Christ had multiplied.[12]

We looked in every nook and cranny of that room, and when we had gathered the last bill we could find, we counted them and there were thirteen dollar bills.

Knowing God had done a miracle, we believed there must be one more dollar bill which we had missed.

Finally, we moved the old icebox away from the wall, and there was the fourteenth dollar bill, exactly the amount we needed to meet our obligation on time! God had performed a material miracle to meet our need.

He created our material world and His power can touch that world the same as it touches the spiritual world.

We had sown dollars. Now we were reaping them. And before that month ended, our harvest was abundantly more than we had sown.

Expecting Results

Elijah visited a widow in Zarephath during the famine. She was destitute, preparing to cook her last cake of meal, then she and her son planned to die. Elijah directed her to bake him a cake first!

This seemed selfish and heartless. But when the widow obeyed, it was like a farmer planting the choice seed. That last cake became her seed-cake. It produced a bountiful return — a harvest of much more than she gave to Elijah. Her *bin of flour was not used up, nor did* her *jar of oil run dry.*[13]

That was God's material blessing in a woman's life.

One of the greatest hindrances to material blessings for women is when they say: "Oh, I give because I want to. As a woman, I don't expect anything in return."

Suppose a widow with a farm, said: "I sow these fields each spring because I love to plant them, but I expect no harvest." How long could she survive?

A good woman farmer expects a good harvest. Good seeds always produce good returns for women the same as they do for men.

Facts for Females

Each time you set aside your *firstfruits* or seed-gift to plant in the Lord's work, remember these three fundamental facts:

FACT I

As a woman believer, keep your expectations only on the Lord. He alone is your supply, your only source.

My God shall supply all of your needs.[14]

He is the life of every good seed.

He is the creator of all wealth.

He is the source from which your abundant return must flow.

How excellent is Your lovingkindness, O God! therefore ... people shall be abundantly satisfied ... for with You is the fountain (source) *of life.*[15]

As a woman, when you plant your seed-money and anticipate your increased harvest, do not limit your increase to your employer's willingness to raise your salary, or to an increased interest or dividend on your savings or securities, or to an enlarged paycheck, annuity, a better job, *etc.*

God is the source of your supply. He may use those means, but He is not limited to them. Keep your eyes on Him — not on the means He might use. He, and He alone is the source of your expectations.

FACT II

When you as a woman believer, plant your seed-money in the Lord's work, remember to plant with an increased return in mind. In other words, plant objectively.

Your giving must be productive. Jesus said, *It is more blessed* (productive) *to give than to receive.*[16] If your giving does not produce a return of more than you give, how will the Lord's work be financed tomorrow?

Every time you invest in God's work of reaching lost souls, you are planting seed-money so that you may reap more than you give — so that you may sow more the next time and then reap a greater return for the Lord's work.

This takes vision and it demands faith. This calls for action and for believing. This is why tradition has developed the easier way of keeping and losing.

FACT III

When you as a woman believer, sow your seed money in God's work, expect an increased return.

Expect a Miracle.

Expect more back than you gave.

Expect God to fulfill His promise.

Expect a financial harvest.

Expect divine intervention to return to you more than you gave.

Expect God to make His word good to YOU as a woman believer.

Without faith it is impossible to please Him, for anyone who comes to God must believe that He is a rewarder.[17]

There can be no miracle without expectation.

After you have sown your seed-money, expect growth. And keep your expectation on God as your only source because, as Paul said, *God gives the increase.*[18]

Once you have acted in faith on His word of promise, you have every right to expect a miracle return.   Once you have sown, expect to reap. Without expectation, faith is dead.

God's law of sowing and reaping is unfailing.

God wills material prosperity for *The Woman Believer* who chooses to be part of His plan to bless humanity.

Material Blessings for Women

God has given to (The Woman Believer) exceeding great and precious promises.[19]

Those who seek the Lord lack no good thing.[20]

My God shall supply all your need.[21]

The Lord will open to you his good treasure.[22]

The blessing of the Lord brings wealth.[23]

The Lord shall command the blessing upon you ... in all that you set your hand to.

The condition is to *only believe*[24] the gospel message that Christ redeemed you from your sins and from their effects. *God took the sinless Christ and poured into Him your sins. Then in exchange, He poured God's goodness into you.*[25]

That puts you in right standing with God so that His best, physically, spiritually and materially, can be yours.

1.	De.28:11	9.	De.8:18	18.	1Co.3:6
2.	De.28:8	10.	Mal.3:10	19.	2Pe.1:4
3.	De.28:4	11.	Ex.16:17-18	20.	Ps.34:10
4.	De.28:5	12.	Jn.6:12-13	21.	Ph.4:19
5.	De.28:1	13.	1K.17:9-16	22.	De.28:12
6.	2Co.9:8	14.	Ph.4:19	23.	Pr.10:22 NIV
7.	2Co.9:11	15.	Ps.36:7-9	24.	He.11:6
8.	2Co.9:13	16.	Ac.20:35	25.	2Co.5:21 LB
		17.	He.11:6		

Chapter 25

PROMISES FOR PROSPERITY

IT IS GOD'S WILL that every woman be re-born to the abundant life. From the moment you accept Jesus Christ by faith, you become a royal daughter in God's family with all of the legal and equal rights of any family member. Realizing that produces a re-birth of self-worth in you.

God wants you, *The Woman Believer,* to enjoy His best. To help you appropriate His material promises, I have personalized them for you.

He challenges you to bring of whatever money you have to Him, and to *prove Him with it now ... and see if He will not open you the windows of heaven, and pour you out a blessing, that there shall not be room enough to receive.*[1]

For the Lord God says ... the bin of flour shall not be used up, nor shall the jar of oil run dry.[2]

For the earth is the Lord's and the fullness thereof.[3]

You shall make your way prosperous, and you shall have good success.[4]

Seek first the expansion of God's kingdom worldwide, and all these things shall be added to you.[5]

The Lord is your shepherd, you shall not want.[6]

No good thing will He withhold from them that walk uprightly.[7]

Blessed are you when you fear the Lord, when you delight greatly in His commandments. Wealth and riches shall be in your house.[8]

The silver is Mine, and the gold is Mine.[9] All the earth is Mine.[10] The land is Mine.[11] Every beast of the forest is Mine, and the cattle on a thousand hills.[12] How excellent is your lovingkindness, O God! therefore ... people put their trust under ... Your wings. They shall be abundantly satisfied ... for with You is the fountain (source) of life.[13]

O Lord, how manifold are Your works ... the earth is full of Your riches ... You open Your hands, they are filled with good.[14]

Those who seek Me early shall find me. Riches and honor are with Me; enduring riches and righteousness ... that I may cause those who love Me to inherit wealth; and I may fill their treasuries.[15]

Blessed are you, Lord God ... for all that is in the heaven and in the earth is Yours ... Both riches and honor come from You.[16]

Walk in God's ways ... that you may prosper in all that you do and wherever you turn yourself.[17]

Blessed is the Lord, who daily loads you with benefits.[18]

A faithful person shall abound with blessings.[19]

Keep ... the words of this covenant ... that you may prosper in all that you do.[20]

I am come that you may have life, and that you may have it more abundantly.[21]

The world of abundance that God has created all around you is proof that He wills material abundance and blessing for *The Woman Believer* who follows Christ the same as for the man believer.

The woman believer should read this following verse like this:

There is no (woman) who has left house, or brothers, or sisters, or father, or mother, ... or lands, for My sake, and the gospel's, but (she) shall receive a hundredfold now in this time, houses and loved ones and lands ... and in the world to come eternal life.[22]

God wills material blessing for you as *The Woman Believer* so that you may bring part of your wealth and dedicate it to share the gospel with others.

When you do this, you become a co-worker with God — a missionary or messenger or preacher just as much as the one who gives the message.

You not only receive a messenger's reward; but God miraculously returns your money ... *good measure, pressed down, running over.*[23]   It is His covenant. He cannot break it.

Always remember: God's prosperity is for

you, *The Woman Believer* — spiritually, physically
and materially.

1.	Mal.3:10	9.	Hag.2:8	17.	1K.2:3
2.	1K.17:14	10.	Ex.19:5	18.	Ps.68:19
3.	1Co.10:26	11.	Le.25:23	19.	Pr.28:20
4.	Jos.1:8	12.	Ps.50:10	20.	De.29:9
5.	Mt.6:33 RV	13.	Ps. 36:7-9	21.	Jn.10:10
6.	Ps.23:1	14.	Ps.104:24,28	22.	Mk.10:29-30
7.	Ps.84:11	15.	Pr.8:17-18,21	23.	Lu.6:38
8.	Ps.112:1,3	16.	1Chr.29:10-12		

PART VI

BY T.L. OSBORN

IF I
WERE A
WOMAN

GOD'S WOMAN

by T.L. Osborn

God's woman,
  She has been redeemed;
God's woman,
  She has new esteem.

  She's come alive,
  She's on the rise,
  She has a choice.
  She has a voice.

God's Woman,
  With a mission and a call;
God's Woman,
  With a vision for us all.

  She's anointed. She's a witness.
  She's appointed. She is gifted.
  Christ is her identity
  Of dignity and destiny.

The blood of Christ removed her shame.
  Now she acts in Jesus' name.
The power of the Holy Ghost,
  Has sent her to the uttermost.

God's Woman,
  Of faith and hope and power.
God's Woman,
  With life and love this hour.

"Practice being aware of Jesus alive and at work in and through you, making you all that God planned for you to be. That is the lifestyle of The Woman Believer."

IF I WERE A WOMAN, I would embrace total salvation and never acquiesce before any doctrine, teaching or cultural tradition which impugns me or denies my worthiness as Christ's witness, His representative, His ambassador or His co-worker in any private or public ministry to which He leads or inspires or calls me.

Are class and sex discriminations of archaic Bible cultures to be imposed today? Only upon women? Are women redeemed, but kept at a distance? Restored, but unworthy to speak for Christ who justified them? Are their sins forgiven, but held against them, while the sins of *man*kind are expunged forever?

No royal daughter of God's family should allow religious dogmas to confine her in subservience, submission, subjection or subordination.

Chapter 26

THE REDEEMED WOMAN

WHEN WOMEN UNDERSTAND their total salvation and recognize their own equality in God's plan, they usually become involved in some kind of personal or public ministry to needy people. Discovering their individual dignity and their destiny in God's redemptive plan emancipates them forever from the primitive bias of sex discrimination which has so impeded women in Christian ministry.

Chauvinistic manipulation of womankind has permeated the religions of the world for many long centuries. The influence of medieval cultures and of archaic dogmas still dictates stubborn suppression of women in the church.

But contrary to religious female subjugation, the message of the gospel — Christ's message of good news is that, when redemption was accomplished, women the same as men were justified and restored to God as though no sin had ever been committed.

To continue the doctrine of female inferiority and of her ineligibility for certain ministries in which only men are worthy to serve, is to mitigate the redemptive work of Christ on a sexual basis.

The redemption of humankind through Christ's vicarious death, burial and resurrection restored both women and men to God. To argue that womankind is forever disqualified for public ministry

and suited only for subservient roles, while
exonerating mankind from all effects of sin, is to
limit Christ's redemptive work for women, while
embracing its total effect for men. This is inter-
preting the redemptive sacrifice of Christ on a sexual basis.

Redemption, therefore, being a fact, if I were
a woman, I would no longer permit outdated traditions from medieval societies to incriminate me as
a royal daughter in God's family, nor to restrain
me from my highest possible achievement and fulfillment in whatever level of private or public
ministry God put in my heart to exercise.

Chapter 27

MAKING OF THE WOMAN BELIEVER

I WILL POUR out My Spirit on all flesh; your sons and your daughters shall prophesy ...

And also on My menservants and on My maidservants I will pour out My Spirit in those days ... Whoever calls on the name of the Lord shall be saved.[1]

If I were a woman with a desire to obey Christ and to be His witness[2] in whatever capacity I felt He inspired or called or led me, I would accept Joel's prophecy as being for me; I would act upon Christ's words and allow Him to speak and to minister through me to the fullest extent by which He could use me.

If I were a woman I would not permit myself, or my status, or my ministry as a woman to be demeaned or depreciated to a subservient level by the traditions and dictums of male clergymen.

The Beginning

In the beginning, *God created man in His own image ... male and female created He them.*[3]

From the dawn of human history, God's ideal was a man and a woman, side by side; sharing with each other, working and living together, loving and playing together — companionship, teamwork, inti-

macy, comaradery, partnership. God never created
womankind to be the slave or the servant of
mankind.

Marriage is the happy state of one woman and
one man sharing life together in love and in mutual
respect. That was God's original and beautiful
dream.

Adam and Eve esteemed each other. They were
one flesh, one kind of being. But they disobeyed
God and were consequently driven from the garden
of Eden because they could no longer live in God's
presence after they had sinned. They became the
slaves of Satan whom they chose to obey, and their
troubles began.

The Problem

Lust began to replace love. Greed and evil superseded good. Because of man's fallen nature and
his larger physique, he subjugated woman for his
own purposes. Instead of loving her as his own
flesh, he manipulated her for monetary advantage
and for his physical pleasure.

Deterioration and death resulted and were in-
bred into all succeeding generations. *The wages of
sin is death.*[4] *As by one person, sin entered into the
world, and death by sin; so death passed upon all
persons, for all have sinned.*[5]

Theology blames womankind for the fall of
humanity because Eve was first to partake of the
forbidden fruit. But it could be argued as well that
Adam disobeyed God before Eve did by allowing
Satan to enter the garden which God told him not
only to *dress*, or to *till*, but also to *keep.*[6]

(Hebrew: To hedge, to guard, to protect.)   Adam was given dominion over Eden but he neglected to exercise his rights — and Satan entered.

Responding to Satan's ruse, *the woman saw that the tree was good ... she took of the fruit thereof, and did eat.* Then the Bible adds, *and Eve gave also to her husband with her; and he did eat, and the eyes of them both were opened.*[7] Adam who was *with her,* also *did eat.* So, not only did Adam neglect to *keep* the garden; he also ate of the forbidden fruit *with* Eve.

It is prejudicial to incriminate Eve and to blame womankind for this original sin, when Adam committed the same transgression. And we must remember that there is also another woman, Mary, whom we can acclaim for our salvation from sin. It was through Mary's obedience that the Savior of the world was born.[8] So if we blame a woman, Eve, for the deterioration of humankind, let us acclaim a woman, Mary, for the redemption of humankind.

If I were a woman, I would no longer see myself as demeaned because of a woman's disobedience.   Rather, I would see myself as redeemed because of a woman's obedience.

The Restoration

Thank God, redemption was provided for both womankind and for mankind.[9] Both have been justified and restored to God through Christ's death and sacrifice in which He endured the judgment of all sins[10] — those of women as well as those of men.

Womankind, as well as mankind, was restored

to God to share His life, to do His work and to be
His instrument, without social, racial or sexual
distinction. On the cross, Jesus abolished female
subservience forever.[11] But women often still bear
the stigma of inferiority because theologians have
not emphasized the fact that Christ's redemption restored womankind to her original place with God,
the same as mankind was restored.

Two thousand years ago, Jesus liberated every
believing woman and man. But outdated church tradition still holds womankind responsible for the fall
of humanity, and forbids them to preach or to
teach. This restriction is based on a few remarks
made by Paul[12] which are as inapplicable today as
it would be to require church members to sell their
possessions because they did it in the primitive
church.[13]

Since humanity has been redeemed, Paul says,
*We are no longer Jews or Greeks or slaves or free
or even men or women, but we are all the same — we
are Christians; we are one in Christ Jesus.*[14]

If I were a woman, I would embrace my total
salvation and never again acquiesce before any doctrine or teaching or cultural tradition which impugns
me or which diminishes my worthiness as Christ's
witness, as His representative, as His ambassador
or as His co-worker in any private or public ministry to which He calls me.

1.	Jl.2:28-32	7.	Ge.3:6-7	11.	Ep.2:15-19
2.	Ac.1:8	8.	Mt.1:21	12.	1Co.14:34
3.	Ge.1:27		Lu.1:28-38		1Ti.2:11-12
4.	Ro.6:23	9.	1Pe.2:24	13.	Ac.4:34-35; 5:1
5.	Ro.5:12	10.	Ro.5:6	14.	Ga.3:28 LB
6.	Ge.2:15		2Co.5:21		

Chapter 28

THE WOMAN PACESETTER

IS IT SIGNIFICANT to you as a woman believer that Mary Magdalene was commissioned by Christ *to find the disciples and to tell them, "I have seen the Lord!"*? Is it significant that *she gave them His message?*[1]

It should be encouraging to women believers that Mary Magdalene was there when Christ arose. He had told His followers that He would rise, but the men were not there. Mary went to the sepulchre, and as a result, she visited with her risen Lord and was chosen by Him to be the first messenger of His resurrection.

And remember: The resurrection is the heartbeat of Christianity. *If Christ be not raised, your faith is vain; you are yet in your sins.*[2] The salvation of every person is linked to the belief and confession *that God has raised Jesus from the dead.*[3]

Jesus said to Mary: *Go to my brethren, and say to them, I ascend to my Father, and your Father; and to My God, and your God.*[4] He sent a woman to proclaim the most vital message of God's redemptive work, to the apostles themselves.

If I were a woman, I would comprehend, by that action, that the ministry of winning souls, of witnessing for Christ and of proclaiming His message is as much for women as it is for men.

1. Jn.20:17-18 LB
2. 1Co.15:17
3. Ro.10:9
4. Jn.20:17

Daisy gives keynote address at her National Conference in Adelaide, Australia.

Daisy and T.L.'s daughter, LaDonna, preaches at International Gospel Center at Tulsa, OK, where she is the pastor.

Chapter 29

THE SPIRIT FILLED WOMAN

THE POWER OF the Holy Spirit was poured out upon the early believers — both men and women together. Christ said to His followers, *You shall receive power after the Holy Spirit comes upon you and you shall be My witnesses ... to the end of the earth.*[1] Did that promise include women believers?

Jesus used the word *witness*, in a culture where, under Judaism, women were forbidden from any court of law, and were inadmissible as witnesses. Yet, having redeemed and restored them to God, Jesus qualified women forever, as *His witnesses* anywhere on earth.

If women should not be witnesses of Christ's resurrection, why should they have been included in the account? *These all continued with one accord, in prayer and supplication, with the women.*[2]

The women were there on the day of Pentecost. The women as well as the men received the Holy Spirit.

Considering the suppressed state of womanhood under Judaism, it is no accident that the Holy Spirit specifies, *with the women ... and they were all filled* so that they could all be *Christ's witnesses,* sharing His good news with the world.

Why was the Holy Spirit given to the women? To be My *witnesses,*[3] Jesus said. The word He used can mean to preach, to teach, to tell, to speak, to prophesy, to demonstrate, to work miracles, to give proof of His resurrection in the form of testimony or of evidence.

Were the men filled with the Holy Spirit to go forth and to preach the gospel with power? Were the women filled with the same Holy Spirit to stay in the house and to be silent?

If I were a woman, I would conclude that the power of the Holy Spirit in my life is to make me an effective *witness* for Christ in any way that He might lead or inspire or call me in private or public ministry.

I do not mean that I would practice leaving behind my household, my husband, or my children to carry the gospel abroad (although men and fathers have done this, without hesitation and without the slightest thought of neglect or desertion, for centuries).

I mean that, if I were a woman, I would respond to God's inspiration or guidance or calling upon my life, with the same confidence and authority that any man is expected to possess (resolving equitably with my spouse, any family problems or challenges or responsibilities which might be involved).

If I were a woman, I would resolve to never allow ecclesiasticisms, dogmas or doctrines to smother, to stifle or to suppress the calling of God and the anointing of the Holy Spirit in my life as Christ's representative and as His *witness*.

1.   Ac.1:8
2.   Ac.1:14
3.   Ac.1:8

Chapter 30

THE COMMISSIONED WOMAN

JESUS COMMANDED, *Go to all the world and preach the gospel to every creature.*[1] Was that command intended for believers of all races, all colors, both sexes?

He said, *These signs shall follow them that believe.*[2] Did that include Christ's female disciples the same as it did His male disciples?

Jesus said, *Those who believe on Me, the works that I do shall they do also.*[3] Did that include women believers as well as men believers?

When you understand the subjugation of womankind before redemption, you see why the Bible specifies that the men were *with the women* when the Holy Spirit came.

This experience electrified the community. Crowds from many nations assembled to witness this strange event in Jerusalem. It astounded and shocked them that *the women* were in the midst of it all.

The Prophecy Fulfilled

Peter explained that this was the fulfillment of a major prophecy. He said in essence: *Look, we are not drunk as some of you suppose; this is the fulfillment of Joel's prophecy, I will pour out My Spirit upon all flesh: Your sons and your daughters shall prophesy.*[4]

Then Peter continued to quote: *And on My menservants and on My maidservants I will pour out My Spirit in those days and they shall prophesy.*[5]

Peter's explanation: "Jewish tradition has discriminated against women. You marvel that the women are receiving the same power as the men. Your own prophet Joel, said this would happen. He predicted that God would pour out His Spirit upon *all flesh;* that His *sons,* His *daughters,* His *servants* and His *handmaidens* would receive power and would prophecy."

A new day had begun. Womankind had been restored to God the same as mankind, and they recognized their equality as authorized *witnesses* of Christ and as anointed proclaimers of the gospel.

Believers were added to the Lord, multitudes both of men and women.[6]

At that time there was a great persecution against the church ... and they who were scattered abroad went everywhere preaching the word.[7]

Both *men and women* were active in *preaching the word. Saul* (the great persecutor of those who proclaimed Christ) *was like a wild man, going everywhere to devastate the believers, even entering private homes and dragging out men and women, and jailing them.*[8] Would Saul have arrested the women, had they not been spreading Christ's message too?

If I were a woman, I would resolve to exercise every ministry with which Christ would anoint and inspire me, to be part of spreading His message of good news to needy people.

1.	Mk.16:15	4.	Ac.2:15-17	7.	Ac.8:1,4
2.	Mk.16:17	5.	Ac.2:18	8.	Ac.8:3 LB
3.	Jn.14:12	6.	Ac.5:14		

Whether in tête-a-tête sessions or during national TV interviews, Daisy considers the successful husband-wife-team, which she and T.L. exemplify, one of the most vital elements in a lifestyle of following Christ and of representing Him in a hurting world.

Chapter 31

THE ISSUE OF EQUALITY

ALTHOUGH EARLY CHRISTIANS came to realize that Christ's redemption lifted them from primitive racial and sexual discrimination, when the new believers began to organize their communities, delicate and painful issues began to surface.

The new liberty and equality amidst the early believers were tested not only by the seating arrangement, but by many procedures in their new meeting places, where they were still being influenced by Jewish class and gender distinctions.

There were six separate courts in the Jewish Temple: 1) The Court of Gentiles or foreigners, on the outside; 2) the Sacred Enclosure where no Gentile could enter without the penalty of death; 3) the restricted Court of Women; 4) the Court of Israel for male Jews; 5) the Court restricted to Priests; and 6) the House of God.

End of Sex Discrimination

In redemption, all partitions were eliminated. Every believer, regardless of race, sex or other distinction, stood on equal ground before God and could come into His holy presence; all divisions were obliterated between Jews and Gentiles,[1] between men and women,[2] and between priests and the laity.[3]

But it was not easy for those Jewish male believers to accept this new equality of womankind.

Though they believed that Jesus was the Messiah, they clung to many *traditions, teaching for doctrines the commandments of men.*[4]

Some refused certain meats.[5] Others practiced circumcision.[6] And the matter of women inside the church was, for them, a new situation which they found very difficult to accept.

The Persistent Conflict

There had always been a restricted Women's Court. The men had always been the ones who occupied the principal section. Only males had been permitted to officiate in spiritual worship, to conduct meetings, to debate and to discuss current issues, business affairs, community problems, or to officiate in ceremonies. (In many countries women are still segregated in the public worship services.)

In these new Christian communities, male Jews who had become believers in Christ, grudgingly conceded their superiority over women. It strained their traditional concept of male prominence in God's house for them to admit women into the sanctuary. But the idea of women speaking publicly, or teaching, was simply not acceptable. They rationalized that male superiority should never be expected to sustain such an indignity as that would impose.

Gentile women were never tolerated closer to the Temple than in the Court of the Gentiles — outside the actual Temple. Jewish women had always been restricted within the Women's Court. But now, Jewish — and even Gentile women were permitted inside the sanctuary to see, to hear and even to participate in the worship — something which seemed to many male Jewish believers to be intolerable or even sacrilegious.

But this new status in Christ was intriguing to the women, many of whom were outspoken, or boisterous, or just curious.   The fact of male-female equality in these new communities strained their spiritual understanding of Christ's redemption to the point of precipitating agonizing debates and heart-searching "spiritual" double-talk.

But has not the modern world progressed beyond such archaic scruples?

1.	Ro.10:12	5.	Ac.10:14	6.	Ac.15:1-3
2.	Ga.3:28		Ac.11:8-9		Ga.6:12-13
3.	Re.1:6		Ac.15:29		
4.	Mk.7:7-8		1Co.8:4-7		
	Ti.1:14		1Ti.4:3-4		

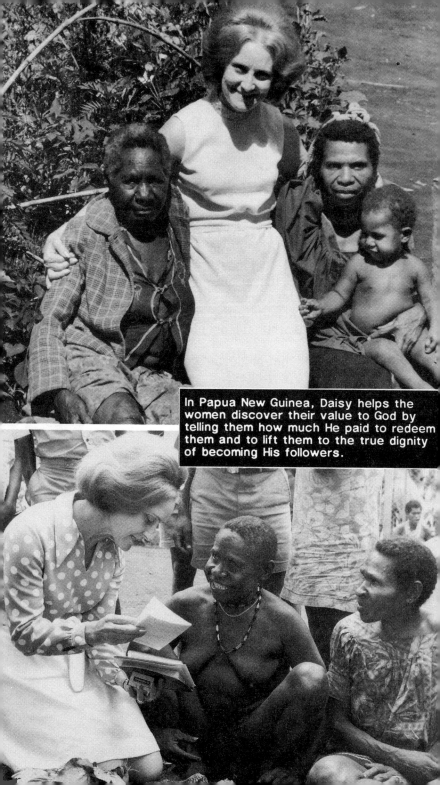

In Papua New Guinea, Daisy helps the women discover their value to God by telling them how much He paid to redeem them and to lift them to the true dignity of becoming His followers.

Chapter 32

THE NEW GENERATION

IN TODAY'S SOCIETY, does church discipline require Christian hosts to wash a traveler's feet, because it was the custom in Bible days? Do the guardians of church tradition earn their living *by the sweat of their face*,[1] as God said, or do they enjoy air conditioning?

Can sophisticated, educated, Christian women today continue to acquiesce in subservient roles of ministry, and remain silent about giving God's message to the world? In what other areas of society would modern women submit to primitive traditions imposed by antique religious dogmas which oblige them to conform to the customs of past centuries?

The Cost of Silence

The commission of Christ is to share the good news with *every creature.* Women represent two-thirds (if not more) of the body of Christ. More millions would hear the gospel if women who prepare themselves and who desire to obey Christ's call, would become active as public witnesses of Christ and as proclaimers of His gospel.

Why should the traditional church insist upon a doctrine that sequesters Christian women and restrains them from public ministry about Christ, based on two or three cloistered statements made concerning women of an ancient culture?[2]

Prominent scholars agree that the application of these verses to women of all times would contradict Paul's own revelation of redemption.

The "profound" church father, Tertullian, pontificated: "No woman is allowed to speak in church, or even to teach, to baptise or to discharge any *man's* function, much less to take upon herself the *priestly* office." (Emphasis mine.)

But Peter said, *You* (meaning women the same as men) *are ... a royal priesthood.*[3] And John adds, *Jesus Christ has made us* (women as well as men) *kings and priests to God.*[4]

Should church disciplinarians continue to insist upon the discrimination of women, restricting them from public ministry?

Is it not more important to the church that all believers — male and female, become active witnesses, confessors, testifiers or proclaimers of the good news to *every creature* and by every means possible, without restraint based on gender?

To maintain this quaint custom of ministerial discrimination against women believers in the church today — a custom inappropriate to modern society, seems prejudicial to me.

Millions of Moslem women, by their own religious culture, can only be addressed by a woman.

If I were a woman, I would embrace the good news that any redeemed woman has Christ's authority to be His witness, His co-worker, and His messenger anywhere and to anyone, privately or publicly — *to the uttermost part of the earth.*[5]

The Winning Woman

In progressive societies, women and men are educated equally. Women are as accomplished and as professional in the fields of business, of science, of medicine, of education and of politics as men are. Nations are governed by women. Some of the largest business institutions on earth are created, owned and/or presided over by women.

Women had a great share in God's work throughout the Bible, despite being bought and sold like human chattel, restricted from the place of worship, and generally deprived of education. Yet many of them took their places in history among the heroes of all times.

The conquests of believing women have been included in countless Biblical and historical documents despite the prejudicial scrutiny of male scribes who flinched at the mention of their gallantry and of their courage. Imagine the undocumented and the untold triumphs of women of Bible times, whose exploits shall never be known, because chauvinistic scribes could not bring themselves to record them for posterity.

The Encouragement

There is a sufficient record preserved in the Bible, and in church history, to motivate and to encourage any woman today who believes in the redemption of Christ for her own life.

The last person at the cross where Christ was crucified was a woman.[6]

The first person at the tomb of Jesus was a woman.[7]

The first person to proclaim the message of our Lord's resurrection was a woman.[8]

The first person to share the gospel with the Jews was a woman.[9]

Among those who attended the first recorded prayer meeting after Christ's resurrection were women.[10]

Among the first to be endued with the power of the Holy Spirit, as witnesses for Christ, were women.[11]

The first persons to greet the Christian missionaries in Europe — Paul and Silas — were women.[12]

The first European convert to believe on Christ was a woman.[13]

1.	Ge.3:19	5.	Ac.1:8	10.	Ac.1:14
2.	1Co.14:34	6.	Mk.15:47	11.	Ac.2:4, Ac.1:8
	1Ti.2:11-12	7.	Jn.20:1	12.	Ac.16:13
3.	1Pe.2:9	8.	Mt.28:8	13.	Ac.16:14
4.	Re.1:6;5:10	9.	Lu.2:37-38		

Chapter 33

LIMITATIONS OR FREEDOM

WHAT LIMITS ARE appropriate for women in Christian ministry today?

Contemporary tradition conveniently approves a woman teaching a Sunday School class, or witnessing in a subdued way of what Christ has done for her. She may be a missionary, or minister in a house. She may prepare the food and serve tables at church affairs (although the men did this in the early church).[1]

Why should a believing woman be forbidden to publicly preach or to teach the gospel of Jesus Christ as His living witness?

If a woman can go to a supermarket, to a park, to a store or to a sidewalk and witness of Christ, may she quote scriptures to corroborate her witness? If so, how many Bible verses may she cite before her witness would be considered to be "preaching" or "teaching"?

If she may witness to one unconverted person, may she witness to two, or to ten, or to a hundred, or to a thousand at the same time? At what point does the number of her listeners exceed the limit for a woman and oblige her to call for a man to do the speaking?

If she may witness to an unconverted person in a subway or in a private house, may she witness to one or to many in a public hall which she might rent, or under a tent which she might erect?

If she may witness along a footpath or a sidewalk, suppose a group gathers. May she step up on a boulder, or a box or a chair in order to be heard? Could she mount a platform? How loud may she speak before she is out of order?

If she may pray for one unbeliever, may she pray for two, or ten, or a hundred at a time? How many is too many for a woman?

If she may witness, may she teach or preach?

Should modern Christian women submit to the restraints of antiquated cultural sex discrimination which denies them equality in public ministry for Christ? If I were a woman, I would not.

Do believing women have the Biblical right to allow their witness for Christ to be suppressed? Can they surrender to silence in Christian ministry because of Paul's statements, when so many scholars agree that his remarks have been taken out of their cultural context, misconstrued, and unjustly applied to women of this epoch?

If I were a woman, I would not surrender to the repression of my ministry. If someone told me that I could not publicly teach or preach about Jesus, I would thank God for my voice and for my right of choice to obey my Lord as His witness, despite the demeaning ruse of supressionists in the church.

The Field — the World

Informed women know that the only area where they have been forbidden to *teach* and to *speak* is inside the church buildings.[2] (The Greek word which Paul used means "a religious congregation", "assembly", "Jewish synagogue", *etc.*)

Even if women acquiesce to this primitive restraint inside the churches, there is no scriptural limits on the ministry of a Christian woman outside the church walls.   That is where sharing the good news is most needed and most effective.

Daisy asks: "Why should women feel discouraged in their ministries when restricted to silence inside the church building?   *The world is our field,* Jesus said."[3]

She advises: "Rather than to publicly remain silent about Christ and His love, let believing women *lift up their eyes and look on the fields*[4] of the whole world, out where they can obey their Lord without contravening theological scruples about women.

"If women submit to what Paul is alleged to have taught about being silent *inside* the church building, let them obey what Christ clearly taught about being His witness *outside* the church — *to the end of the earth."*[5]   I heartily agree with Daisy.

It is not wrong for believing women to go out where the people are, to give Christ's message to the world, privately or publicly, and to win souls to Him.

There is a new army of spiritual Joans of Arc who recognize their freedom and their equality in redemption. They are on the rise, worldwide, and they are giving the good news to millions throughout the world who might not be reached without the ministry of these courageous believing women. This is progress in Christian ministry.

The Female Awakening

Should we not *rightly divide the word of truth*?[6] Should educated Christian women acquiesce to sex discrimination in God's work and bow to religious subservience because of Paul's words which have been misconstrued to imply a contradiction of all of his own revelation and teaching about the redemption of womankind the same as mankind?

Are scriptures to be qualified sexually? Are the class and sex distinctions of archaic Bible cultures to be imposed today? Only upon the women? Was the redemption of womankind limited? Was she redeemed, but kept at a distance? Is she justified before God, but considered "unqualified" to speak for Christ who restored her? Were her sins forgiven? Forgotten by God? But remembered by men? — while the sins of mankind were expunged forever?

The Believing Woman

Should a woman who believes in redemption, and who desires to share the good news, allow men or systems to forbid her from doing what Jesus commissioned her to do?

Can believing women afford to permit persons, or boards, or institutions to limit or to stifle their witness for Christ who chose a woman to proclaim the greatest message in Christianity — that He is risen?

Are Christian women to be silent in God's work today when so many women in the Bible were His messengers?

Is it possible for a believing woman to use Paul's words as an excuse for her own lack of courage to become involved in giving Christ's message to the world?

Can believing women afford to bow to discrimination in the church world, while in the secular world their equality is a fact of life?

Should Christian women be considered inferior or subservient in the church, while their equality is evidenced in business, in science, in medicine, in politics and in government?   Should primitive sex-discrimination be imposed only upon the women in today's church?   Is any such cultural yoke imposed upon Christian men today?

1.	Ac.6:2-3	4.	Jn.4:35
2.	1Co.14:34	5.	Ac.1:8
3.	Mt.13:38	6.	2Ti.2:15

Daisy Osborn, always radiant and ready for action, devotes her life to inspiring audiences and readers around the world to choose Jesus Christ and to follow Him.

Chapter 34

THE WOMAN I WOULD BE

1. If I were a woman, I would obey Jesus Christ outside the church building — if I felt led or inspired or called to do so, as much as I would tolerate religious tradition inside the church institution.

2. If I were a woman, I would consider myself a Christian, a believer, a follower of Christ, His *witness* and a messenger of His resurrection to *every creature,* to any extent to which I felt led or inspired to act.

3. If I were a woman, I would embrace the fact that Christ lives in me, He serves through me, He speaks through me, He loves and ministers through me; that my body is His body; that He is free to continue His same ministry through me that He exercised in Bible times; that *as God sent Christ into the world, even so Christ sends me into the world.*[1]

4. If I were a woman, I would do what Christ told believers to do even if I was criticized or misjudged for doing it. Christ suffered reproach for me. *The servant is not above his or her Master.*[2]

5. If I were a woman, I would be one of the wise persons *who heard the sayings of Christ and did them,*[3] building my ministry as His witness upon the rock of faith and action.

6. If I were a woman, filled with the Holy Spirit, I would be Christ's *witness in Jerusalem, in all Judea, in Samaria, and to the end of the earth*[4] to any extent that I felt His call or guidance.

7. If I were a woman and felt God's call to do so, I would act on Joel's prophecy: *I will pour out My spirit upon all flesh; and your sons and your daughters shall prophesy.*[5] I would observe that Peter quoted that prophecy: *On My menservants and on My handmaidens will I pour out of My spirit; and they shall prophesy.*[6] I would be glad that the Hebrew word used by Joel means: Speak or sing by inspiration; to predict or to give a discourse; and that the Greek word used by Peter means: To speak under divine inspiration; to exercise a prophetic office; an inspired speaker.

8. If I were a woman, I would note that Jesus never made a difference between the sexes. I would be impressed by the different women who were associated with His life and ministry. If I felt the desire or call to do so, I would be like the woman of Samaria who, as soon as she believed, evangelized a whole city for Jesus. *The people went out of the city and came to Him ... and many of the Samaritans of the city believed on Him*[7] because of the testimony and the ministry of a woman.

9. If I were a woman, I would remember: 1) that Jesus is my Lord — not Paul or any of the church fathers; 2) that Jesus commissioned women followers (as well as men followers) to *preach the gospel* years before Paul was even converted; 3) that the Holy Spirit endowed women believers (as well as men believers) with *power* to be Christ's

witnesses, years before Paul even believed on Christ; 4) that Jesus Christ, my Savior and Lord, is the one who saved me, empowered me, and called me — not Paul; and 5) that any private or public ministry I might engage in, or any claim of authority to preach or to teach the gospel which I might express is not dependent upon theological tradition, church dogma, or ecclesiastical endorsement, but is based upon the teachings and the commission of my own Lord Jesus Christ, *whom I belong to and whom I serve.*[8]

10.   If I were a woman, I would recognize the full redemptive work of God's grace on my behalf, through Christ; I would embrace my identity as a believer in Christ, redeemed through His shed blood, with all of the inherited rights, privileges and responsibilities of any member, male or female, of God's royal family; and I would never allow any voice, edict, dogma, rule, or doctrine to limit the exercise of my authority as Christ's *witness,* private or public, or to repress my Christian ministry to people anywhere.

The Status — The Message

Any woman can have an unlimited ministry, if she chooses to do what Jesus said to do: To be His *witness,* and to give His message to *every creature.* Her *field is the world.*[9]

Jesus commissions women and men alike to go out where the people are, to the busy boulevards and crossroads of society, out in public halls, theaters, cinemas, parks and ball fields, in houses and mobile homes, under trees, tents, arbors or roofs, to tell the world, *I have seen the Lord* and to give *them His message!*[10]

That is what I would do if I were a woman — one who desires to share Jesus Christ with all those for whom He died.

1. Jn.17:18; 20:21 Paraphrased   5. Jl.2:28   9. Mk.16:15
2. Mt.10:24   6. Ac.2:18   Mt.13:38
3. Mt.7:24   7. Jn.4:39   10. Jn.20:18 LB
4. Ac.1:8   8. Ac.27:23

PART VII

CONFESSIONS
FOR
WOMEN

NO WOMAN can rise above her own thoughts and her own words. If she talks defeat, fear, subservience, failure, anxiety, sickness, inferiority, unbelief, she predestines herself to live on that level.

Whatever God has said about you as a believing child of His, you can say about yourself, and you will become God's kind of woman.

The promises of God become real and living to you only as you embrace them and confess them. Learn the value of God's word in your heart and on your lips.

If a woman's conversation is foolish, trifling, impractical and disorganized, her life is invariably the same way. A woman's words constantly paint a public picture of her inner self.

Make God's word the standard for your life as *The Woman Believer*. Train yourself to say what He says. Sooner than you can imagine, your life will rise to the level of His word in your heart and on your lips.

Chapter 35

WORD POWER FOR WOMEN

A WOMAN'S WORDS are her standard of faith. They express what she really believes.

Did you realize that multitudes of women fail in life because they talk failure? Those who live in mediocrity and inferiority do so because they think and talk that way about themselves.

Any woman's life invariably goes to the level of her thoughts and of her words. This is a simple fact of life and it explains why only a small percentage of women are really successful in life. Those who talk defeat and think defeat, fail.

The Bible has much to say about a woman's words. It abounds with exciting examples of those who spoke faith.

When you talk right, you train yourself to think right and as a result, you act right.

No woman can rise above her own thoughts and her own words. If she talks defeat, fear, subservience, failure, anxiety, sickness, inferiority, unbelief, she predestines herself to live on that level. This principle is unwavering — inflexible.

If a woman's conversation is foolish, trifling, impractical and disorganized, her life is the same way. A woman's words constantly paint a public picture of her inner self. Jesus said: *Out of the abundance of the heart, the mouth speaks.*[1]

The Woman Believer talks what she believes. The way she talks is the way she thinks and believes in her heart.

If your heart and mind are filled with God's word, you will talk that word. Your confession is your real faith talking. There is no believing that does not express itself in confession.

Jesus demanded that you as a woman, not only believe on Him but that you confess Him before people.[2] *The Woman Believer* has a right to say what God says about her in His word, knowing that He will make it good in her life.

That is what is meant by this verse: *For He has said, I will never leave you, nor forsake you. So that we may boldly say: The Lord is my helper.*[3]

66 Living Confessions for *The Woman Believer*

It is because of what *He has said* that *The Woman Believer* may speak boldly. To help you in your faith, here are 66 living confessions which will help you to appropriate God's promised blessings. (I have adapted these Biblical confessions to women.)

1. Because He has said, *So God created man in His own image; in the image of God He created him; male and female He created them ... Then God saw everything that He had made, and indeed it was very good,*[4] you as a woman *may boldly say,* "I am cre-

ated in God's image in the same way that any man is, and when God saw me as a woman, He saw that I was very good, so I believe I am pleasing to God and that there are no limits upon me as His creation — made in His image."

2.   Because He has said, *I, the Lord, have called you in righteousness, and will hold your hand,*[5] and *Fear not, for I have redeemed you by your name; You are Mine,*[6] you as a woman *may boldly say,* "I am vital and valuable to God because He has called me in righteousness, and therefore I am not afraid of opposition, because the Lord has redeemed me by my own name, and He says, *He will not abandon me ... nor forget the promises He has made,*[7] and He says, *I will never leave you nor forsake you.*"[8]

3.   Because He has said, *The Lord is near to all who call upon Him in truth,*[9] you as a woman *may boldly say,* "The Lord is near to me now, because I call on Him according to the truth of His word."

4.   Because He has said, *You are precious in My sight, you have been honored, and I have loved you ... Fear not, for I am with you,*[10] you as a woman *may boldly say,* "I am precious in God's sight and He honors me because He loves me, He values me and He is with me."

5.   Because He has said, *For all the promises of God in Him are yes, and in Him Amen,*[11] you as a woman *may boldly say,* "All of God's promises are for me as much as they are for any man, because His word is given to all of His children."

6.   Because He has said, *My word that goes forth from My mouth; it shall not return to Me void, but it shall accomplish what I please,*[12] you as a woman *may boldly say,* "What God says about me is now fact. It cannot be reversed. It accomplishes in me what God says about me."

7.   Because He has said, *Indeed I have spoken it; and I will also bring it to pass. I have purposed it; I will also do it,*[13] you as a woman *may boldly say,* "Every word of promise which God has spoken and which is addressed to women believers as well as to men, I accept and claim and act upon because I know that His purpose and His will in and through me as a woman, will be accomplished when I believe His word, because *God is not a man, that He should lie, nor a son of man, that He should repent. Has He said, and will He not do it? Or has He spoken, and will He not make it good?*"[14]

8.   Because He has said, *The Lord has pleasure in the prosperity of His servants,*[15] and *wealth and riches shall be in his (or her) house,*[16] you as a woman *may boldly say,* "Yes, Lord, You take pleasure in blessing me as a woman, with plenty. You are the source of all wealth and riches and You do will them for my house."

9.   Because He has said, *Meditate on God's Law day and night, that you may observe to do according to all that is written in it. For then you will make your way prosperous, and then you will have good success,*[17] you as a woman *may boldly say,* "I do meditate on God's word constantly, so that I may observe what He says to me as a woman believer, and this is why I am confident of success and prosperity in my ministry to the world around me."

10.   Because He has said, *The Lord preserves all who love Him,*[18] you as a woman *may boldly say,* "The Lord constantly preserves me because I do love Him with all of my heart."

11.   Because He has said, *Call to Me, and I will answer you, and show you great and mighty things, which you do not know,*[19] you as a woman *may boldly say,* "I can call upon my Lord and He will respond to my needs because it is His will to show me truths and secrets and achievements which have not been normal or understood or experienced by women, and *I will not grow weary while doing good, for in due season I shall reap if I do not lose heart.*"[20]

12.   Because He has said, *They that seek the Lord shall not lack any good thing,*[21] you as a woman *may boldly say,* "God cannot allow me to lack any good thing. He takes care of my every need, because I do seek Him with all my heart."

13.   Because He has said, *Before you call, I will answer; and while you are yet speaking, I will hear,*[22] you as a woman *may boldly say,* "The Lord is answering my prayer even now; in fact He was already working on the answer before I prayed."

14.   Because He has said, *You shall serve the Lord your God, and He shall bless your bread and your water; and I will take sickness away from the midst of you,*[23] you as a woman *may boldly say,* "Sickness is taken away from me; my bread and my water are blessed, because I am serving the Lord my God."

15. Because He has said, *The eyes of the Lord are on the righteous, and His ears are open to their cry,*[24] you as a woman *may boldly say,* "The Lord is watching over me in all that I think and do and say as His co-worker, and He constantly hears my prayers, because I have received the gift of His righteousness through Jesus Christ."[25]

16. Because He has said, *When the enemy shall come in like a flood, the Spirit of the Lord shall lift up a standard against him,*[26] you as a woman *may boldly say,* "God's Spirit is raising a mighty standard of defense in my behalf at the very time the enemy is heaping his pressure on me. Praise the Lord, my case is in His hands."

17. Because His word says, *Blessed is everyone who fears the Lord, who walks in His ways. When you eat the labor of your hands, you shall be happy, and it shall be well with you,*[27] you as a woman *may boldly say,* "I am a blessed woman because I walk in the ways of my Lord without ever holding back because of my gender, and constant happiness and well-being are mine because I labor in my Christian ministry to people, and my efforts produce fruit and fulfillment."

18. Because He has said, *Your God whom you serve continually, He will deliver you,*[28] you as a woman *may boldly say,* "God is my deliverer in every case, because I constantly serve Him."

19. Because He has said, *The Lord will command the blessing on all to which you set your hand, and He will grant you plenty of goods,*[29] you as a woman *may boldly say,* "God is blessing what I do, and I shall succeed and prosper in whatever I put

my hand to, because God cannot fail to back up His word."

20.   Because He has said, *When you pass through the waters, I will be with you; And through the rivers, they shall not overflow you; when you walk through the fire, you shall not be burned, nor shall the flame scorch you,*[30] you as a woman *may boldly say,* "Whatever problem or crisis or opposition I face shall not be able to stop or destroy me in my commitment to God's plan for my life because He is faithful to make His promise good."

21.   Because He has said, *Fear not; for I am with you: be not dismayed; for I am your God,*[31] you as a woman *may boldly say,* "I am no longer afraid because God is with me now and all the time."

22.   Because He has said, *God has not given us the spirit of fear, but of power and of love and of a sound mind,*[32] you as a woman *may boldly say,* "I am free from all fear and inferiority, for my God has given me power, love and a sound mind."

23.   Because He has said, *No weapon formed against you shall prosper, and every tongue which rises against you in judgment you shall condemn; this is the heritage of the servants* (maid as well as male servants) *of the Lord,*[33] you as a woman *may boldly say,* "No dictim or disparagement or tradition or restraint intended to barricade my way or to restrict my ministry in God's service can ever prosper or succeed against me because of my inheritance as a daughter in God's royal family, and *He is my hiding place; He shall preserve me in trou-*

ble; He shall surround me with songs of deliverance."[34]

24. Because He has said, *The Lord shall fight for you, and you shall hold your peace,*[35] you as a woman *may boldly say,* "I know God is fighting for me because I am holding my peace. I have committed my battle into His hands."

25. Because He has said, *The fear of man brings a snare, but whoever trusts in the Lord shall be safe,*[36] you as a woman *may boldly say,* "I shall never allow myself to be snared by male ecclesiasticisms or rules or traditions designed to limit me in my ministry, because my safety is in trusting my Lord and His promises."

26. Because He has said, *If God be for us, who can be against us?*[37] you as a woman *may boldly say,* "God is for me, and neither people nor circumstances can succeed against me."

27. Because He has said, *You shall know the truth, and the truth shall make you free,*[38] you as a woman *may boldly say,* "I am set free, for I know Jesus who is Truth, and He lives in me."

28. Because His word has said, *The Lord is my strength and my shield; my heart trusted in Him, and I am helped;*[39] you as a woman *may boldly say,* "I am strong and I have protection, because I trust in my Lord and He is helping me now as *my light and my salvation: Whom shall I fear? The Lord is the strength of my life. Though an army should encamp against me, my heart shall not fear; though war should rise against me, in this will I be confident.*"[40]

29.   Because He has said, *I am come that you might have life, and that you might have it more abundantly,*[41] you as a woman *may boldly say,* "I have abundant life dwelling in me now, because I have received Jesus Christ."

30.   Because He has said, *Behold, what manner of love the Father has bestowed upon us* (women believers as well as men believers), *that we should be called the children of God,*[42] you as a woman *may boldly say,* "God's love has made me one of His children and because of that, *He has sent forth the Spirit of His Son into my heart, crying out, 'Abba, Father!' Therefore, I am no longer a slave but a daughter, and if a daughter, then an heir of God through Christ.*"

31.   Because He has said, *He who raised Christ from the dead will also give life to your mortal bodies through His Spirit who dwells in you,*[43] you as a woman *may boldly say,* "God is quickening my mortal body now by the very same Spirit that raised Jesus from the dead, because His Spirit dwells in me; therefore I am free from weakness, sickness, inability and fatigue."

32.   Because He has said, *If the Son makes you free, you shall be free, indeed,*[44] you as a woman *may boldly say,* "Jesus, God's Son has set me free from the bondage of chauvinistic traditions and religious subjugation, as well as from my sins and my diseases, and therefore I am free, indeed, and I have resolved to *not be entangled again with a yoke of bondage.*[45]

33.   Because He has said, *Beloved, I wish above all things that you may prosper and be in*

health, even as your soul prospers,[46] you as a woman *may boldly say*, "I have a right to prosperity and health, because I am prospering in my soul."

34.   Because He has said, *With men it is impossible, but not with God; for with God all things are possible*[47] you as a woman *may boldly say*, "Nothing is impossible for God and a believing woman like me, because God believes in me and He can do anything through me that He can do through any other believer."

35.   Because He has said, *Out of His glorious unlimited resources He gives you the mighty inner strengthening of His Holy Spirit,*[48] you as a woman *may boldly say*, "God's resources are as unlimited in me, a woman believer, as they are in any man, and therefore His resources are the secret of my unlimited strength in the Holy Spirit to do His work, *for it is God who works in me both to will and to do His good pleasure.*"[49]

36.   Because He has said, *Blessed be the Lord who daily loads me with benefits,*[50] you as a woman *may boldly say*, "I praise You Lord, because You are filling my life with Your abundance of blessings and good things."

37.   Because He has said, *Give, and it shall be given to you; good measure, pressed down and running over,*[51] you as a woman *may boldly say*, "The Lord is heaping up my blessings, for I am giving to Him and to His work."

38.   Because He has said, *With His stripes we are healed,*[52] you as a woman *may boldly say*, "Yes, Lord, with Your stripes I am healed now."

God says of His own word: *For I am the Lord. I speak, and the word which I speak shall come to pass.*[53]

You can count on God's word being good. It cannot fail because God cannot fail. The word is God speaking to you as a woman, the same as it speaks to men. It reveals the mind and will of God. It is alive. It abides forever. It shall never pass away. Jesus said, *The scripture cannot be broken.*[54]

39.   Because He has said, *If any of you* (that includes women) *lack wisdom, let him or her ask of God, who gives to all liberally and without reproach, and it will be given,*[55] you as a woman *may boldly say,* "In whatever way my lack of experience may have limited my knowledge or understanding in Christian ministry, God has a limitless supply of wisdom ready for me — and without rebuke or rebuff for my shortcomings, so I can achieve success in His service since *He will instruct me and teach me in the way I should go; He will guide me with His eye.*"[56]

40.   Because He has said, *The Spirit of the Lord is upon Me, because He has anointed Me to preach the gospel to the poor, He has sent Me to heal the brokenhearted, to preach deliverance to the captives and recovering of sight to the blind to set at liberty those who are oppressed, to preach the acceptable year of the Lord,*[57] you as a woman *may boldly say,* "Since I am a woman and since women received the Holy Spirit the same as the men, with the same power and for the same reason,[58] then the Holy Spirit can carry on the same ministry of Christ through me — preaching, healing, delivering,

recovering, and liberating poor, brokenhearted, imprisoned, blind, oppressed and hurting human persons, because He is no more limited or restrained by my gender than He is by my color or by my race."

41.   Because He has said, *I am the Lord that heals you,*[59] you as a woman *may boldly say,* "Yes, Lord, You are the Lord who heals me."

Instead of fearing disease or being frustrated by the threat of illness, *you boldly say,* "The Lord heals me." Believe it. Read it. Ponder it until your heart overflows with it. Then God confirms it.

42.   Because His word says, *There is neither Jew nor Greek, there is neither slave nor free, there is neither male nor female, for you are all one in Christ Jesus,*[60] you as a woman *may boldly say,* "What Jesus accomplished for any man, He accomplished for me, and whatever He can do in and through any man, by the power of the Holy Spirit, He can do in and through me, because we are all one in Christ now, and our race or color or sex no longer distinguishes us in the body of Christ."

43.   Because He has said, *Whoever shall confess me before others, I will confess before my Father,*[61] you as a woman *may boldly say,* "Jesus is confessing me right now to the Father because I am confessing Him before people."

44.   Because He has said, *Yet in all things we are more than conquerors through Him who loved us,*[62] you as a woman *may boldly say,* "No tradition or opposition or denigration of my life or of my ministry for Christ can triumph over me be-

cause I am loved by my Lord who paid to redeem
me to God as His partner, and that love makes me
a conqueror in His service, because *it is God who
arms me with strength, and makes my way perfect;
He makes my feet like the feet of deer, and sets me
on my high places ... giving me the shield of
salvation; being held up by His right hand.*"[63]

45.   Because He has said, *Let the weak say, I
am strong,*[64] you as a woman *may boldly say, "I
can do all things through Christ which strengthens
me."*[65]

46.   Because He has said, *He is able to do ex-
ceedingly abundantly above all that we ask or think,
according to the power that works in us,*[66] you as a
woman *may boldly say,* "The power of God is at
work in me, and His power can do more than I can
imagine because I will not allow His life and virtue
in me to be limited by archaic dictums about women
which *make the word of God of no effect.*"[67]

47.   Because He has said, *Himself took our infirmities, and bore our sicknesses,*[68] you as a
woman *may boldly say,* "I am free from weakness
and disease because they were all carried away by
Jesus Christ on my behalf, in my name."

48.   Because He has said, *Go your way and as
you have believed, so be it done to you,*[69] you as a
woman *may boldly say,* "I can be on my way; I
have prayed and believed; the answer will come just
as I am expecting."

49.   Because He has said, *We have been given
exceeding great and precious promises: That through
these you may be partakers of the divine nature,*[70]

you as a woman *may boldly say,* "God's promises
are for me; they are great and precious, and by
them, I have become a partaker of His divine nature in a measure as unlimited and as complete as
any child of God, male or female, may become."

50. Because He has said, *In my name you shall
cast out devils,*[71] you as a woman *may boldly say,*
"I have power to cast out devils, and when I command them to go in Jesus' name, I believe they obey
me."

51. Because He has said, *Whoever hears these
sayings of Mine, and does them, I will liken to a
wise person whose house is built upon a rock,*[72] you
as a woman *may boldly say,* "I know my Lord
sees me as a wise woman because whatever He
has said that believers can do, I have believed and I
have acted upon without hesitating because of my
gender; I am His follower, His disciple, a believer,
and that is what counts, and that is why I have put
action to my faith,[73] and I am a *doer of the
word,*[74] and the house of my life and ministry is
built upon the rock of His word."

52. Because He has said, *You shall lay hands
on the sick, and they shall recover,*[75] you as a
woman *may boldly say,* "Whenever I lay my hands
on the sick, they begin to recover because I am
acting on God's word."

53. Because He has said, *Be steadfast, immovable, always abounding in the work of the Lord,
knowing that your labor is not in vain in the Lord,*[76]
you as a woman *may boldly say,* "I am resolved to
express myself and to dedicate my best in the
Lord's work — regardless of traditional restraints

and church dogmas which try to interdict my ministry as a woman, because what I do in His name and as His partner, is never in vain, but it always succeeds, and knowing this makes me always steadfast and immovable in His work."

54.   Because He has said, *Seek first the expansion of God's kingdom worldwide and all these things shall be added to you,* you as a woman *may boldly say,* "Everything I need in life is mine, from Christ, because I am involved in God's work of worldwide soulwinning."

55.   Because He has said, *Being confident of this very thing, that He who has begun a good work in you will complete it,*[77] you as a woman *may boldly say,* "I am confident of success in my life and ministry because it is Jesus who saved me, then came to live in me, and it is He who loves and ministers through me so that every good thing He has begun in and through me, He will fulfill it according to His plan and *I have committed it to Him.*"[78]

56.   Because He has said, *There is therefore now no condemnation to those who are in Christ Jesus,*[79] you as a woman *may boldly say,* "I am forever free from all guilt and condemnation before God because I am living in Christ Jesus now."

Make God's word the standard for your life as a woman. Train yourself to say what He says. Sooner than you can imagine, your life will rise to the level of His word in your heart and on your lips.

God is in His word. When you confess it, He
makes it good. You as a woman, become the master
of every situation because God is on your side. You
are aligning yourself on the side of His word. He
takes your part, to confirm His word, and your
enemy goes down in defeat.

57. Because He has said, *You are a chosen generation, a royal priesthood, a holy nation, His own
special people, that you may proclaim the praises of
Him who called you out of darkness into His marvelous light,*[80] you as a woman, may boldly say, "I
am chosen, I am in His royal priesthood, I am holy
and am so special that I am fulfilling His will
when I proclaim His message of love, because He
has called me out of darkness to light so that I
may be His witness."

58. Because He has said, *My God shall supply
all your need according to His riches in glory by
Christ Jesus,*[81] you as a woman *may boldly say,*
"God knows every need I face; He is now supply-
ing for those needs, and my supply is as unlimited
as are the riches of Christ Jesus."

59. Because He has said, *I know your works,
See, I have set before you an open door, and no one
can shut it,*[82] you as a woman *may boldly say,* "My
Lord knows about everything that I do and every
effort that I make, and He has opened as wide a
door of private and public ministry to me as He
has opened for any man, and He is the one *who
opens and no one shuts, and shuts and no one
opens.*"[83]

60. Because He has said, *Resist the devil, and
he will flee from you,*[84] you as a woman *may*

boldly say, "I shall always resist any form of the devil's lies about me as a woman in Christian ministry, and I know that his influence or power can never impede or prevent my service to my Lord, but rather, wherever I go, the devil will flee from before my path."

61.   Because He has said, *I will never leave you, nor forsake you,*[85] you as a woman *may boldly say,* "The Lord is my helper; for *If God be for me, who can be against me?"*[86]

62.   Because He has said, *You are the temple of the living God ... I will dwell in them and walk in them,*[87] and *your body is the temple of the Holy Spirit who is in you,*[88] you as a woman *may boldly say,* "The Lord has come to live in me, so wherever I meet Satan, he must deal with Jesus Christ who is alive in me, and no demon or opposition can defeat Him who is alive and at work in and through me."

63.   Because He has said, *I can do all things through Christ which strengthens me,*[89] you as a woman *may boldly say,* "Nothing is impossible for the Lord and me, because He lives in me as a believer, and it is He who is doing the work even now.

64.   Because He has said, *He who is in you is greater than he who is in the world,*[90] you as a woman *may boldly say,* "God dwells in me[91] so my enemy is unable to stand or to prevail against me or anything that I attempt to do in the name of Him who is my life, because it is Christ who lives in me and who ministers and does His work through me."

65.   Because He has said, *Jesus Christ the same yesterday, and today, and forever,*[92] you as a woman *may boldly say,* "The Lord will do as much for me and through me today as He ever did for or through anyone else, because He is unchanged."

66.   Because He has said, *They overcame him* (Satan, the accuser) *by the blood of the Lamb, and by the word of their testimony,*[93] you as a woman *may boldly say,* "I am an overcomer of Satan and of every trick and lie and device and obstacle which he may use to try to defeat or to hinder me as a woman, because I am redeemed by Christ's blood and I accept God's promises, quoting them as my testimony wherever I go."

* * *

Because He has spoken, you know that you can declare it *boldly.* It will be as He has said, because *there has not failed one word of all His good promise which He promised.*[94]

God has given to you His great and abundant promises[95] in order to reveal to you His will. His testament, His will, His promise, His word are all the same.

In order for any woman to receive any blessing from God, it must come to her through faith. To have faith for any blessing, she must be convinced that such a blessing is God's will for her — that it is promised to her in His word. That is why the Bible says that *faith comes by hearing the word of God.*[96]

As long as a woman has a question about whether or not God wills that she receive something, she will not claim it or appropriate it.

The Bible says to ask for things, believing that we receive them. *Ask in faith, with no doubting. For if you doubt, you are like a wave of the sea driven and tossed by the wind. So let not such a person suppose they shall receive anything from the Lord.*[97]

No woman can be saved until she believes that God loves her and that Christ died for her sins — that it is God's will and desire for her to be saved. She then accepts His gift of new life by faith and she is born again. Salvation is for *whoever will.*[98] It is for you, a woman.

In the same way, if you face any other need, you must be convinced, by the promises of God, that it is His will to meet that need. Otherwise you will not be able to ask in faith.

Religious tradition teaches that you should ask for blessings by praying, "if it be God's will." But when God has clearly promised a blessing, you can know that it is His will for you to ask and to receive that blessing.

God has promised His abundant blessing to every woman who believes on Christ. According to the Bible, Christ's abundance includes His best for you, spiritually, physically and materially. His promises reveal His will for you.

That is why: *Because He has said,* you *may boldly say* the same thing. His words are the faith-building, hope-generating, love-empowering confessions for *The Woman Believer*.

1.	Mt.12:34	35.	Ex.14:14	68.	Mt.8:17
2.	Mt.10:32	36.	Pr.29:25	69.	Mt.8:13
3.	He.13:5-6	37.	Ro.8:31	70.	2Pe.1:4
4.	Ge.1:27,31	38.	Jn.8:32	71.	Mk.16:17
5.	Is.42:6	39.	Ps.28:7	72.	Mt.7:24
6.	Is.43:1	40.	Ps.27:1,3	73.	Ja.2:26
7.	De.4:31 LB	41.	Jn.10:10	74.	Ja.1:22
8.	He.13:5	42.	1Jn.3:1	75.	Mk.16:18
9.	Ps.145:18	43.	Ro.8:11	76.	1Co.15:58
10.	Is.43:4-5	44.	Jn.8:36	77.	Ph.1:6
11.	2Co.1:20	45.	Ga.5:1	78.	2Ti.1:12
12.	Is.55:11	46.	3Jn.2	79.	Ro.8:1
13.	Is.46:11	47.	Mk.10:27	80.	1Pe.2:9
14.	Nu.23:19	48.	Ep.3:16 LB	81.	Ph.4:19
15.	Ps.35:27	49.	Ph.2:13	82.	Re.3:8
16.	Ps.112:1,3	50.	Ps.68:19	83.	Re.3:7
17.	Jos.1:8	51.	Lu.6:38	84.	Ja.4:7
18.	Ps.145:20	52.	Is.53:5	85.	He.13:5-6
19.	Je.33:3		1Pe.2:24	86.	Ro.8:31
20.	Ga.6:9	53.	Eze.12:25,28	87.	2Co.6:16
21.	Ps.34:10	54.	Jn.10:35	88.	1Co.6:19
22.	Is.65:24	55.	Ja.1:5	89.	Ph.4:13
23.	Ex.23:25	56.	Ps.32:8	90.	1Jn.4:4
24.	Ps.34:15	57.	Lu.4:18	91.	1Jn.4:12
25.	Ro.5:17	58.	Ac.1:8,14	92.	He.13:8
26.	Is.59:19	59.	Ex.15:26	93.	Re.12:11
27.	Ps.128:1-2	60.	Ga.3:28	94.	1K.8:56
28.	Da.6:16	61.	Mt.10:32	95.	2Pe.1:4
29.	De.28:8,11	62.	Ro.8:37	96.	Ro.10:17
30.	Is.43:2	63.	Ps.18:32-35	97.	Ja.1:6-7
31.	Is.41:10	64.	Jl.3:10	98.	Jn.3:16
32.	2Ti.1:7	65.	Ph.4:13		Ro.10:13
33.	Is.54:17	66.	Ep.3:20		Re.22:17
34.	Ps.32:7	67.	Mk.7:13		

PART VIII

A
WOMAN'S
BIRTHRIGHT

AS A DAUGHTER in God's family, you belong to royalty and Christ lives at your house.

Every woman needs a source from which to draw strength and power to win in life's struggles.

This book will put the stuff in *The Woman Believer* to triumph over oppression, religious discrimination, inferiority and intimidation.

What can happen to the woman who fails to discover herself in God's redemptive plan?

Salvation is the all-*inclusive* word that embraces every blessing that Jesus provided for women through His death, burial and resurrection.

Now *The Woman Believer* can walk in newness of life, as more than a conqueror, because God always causes her to triumph in Christ.

When a woman accepts Christ, He dwells in her. This is the heritage of women servants of the Lord.

Chapter 36

A WOMAN'S POWER TO WIN

WOMEN WERE CREATED to be winners with God. Failure is never His will for *The Woman Believer*. He never wants her to succumb to defeat.

Insecurity and uncertainty are not God's plan for you as a woman believer. Never settle for mediocrity. Stay identified with Him. That makes you a winner. That is a woman's birthright.

Every woman needs a source from which to draw strength and power to win in life's struggles.

But your adversary, the devil, will seek by every cunning trick he knows, to defeat your claims as a believing woman. He will undermine your rights and your relationship with God, constantly accusing and condemning you, destroying your faith and clouding you with a sense of guilt and inferiority.

Knowledge Brings Freedom

When you do not know God's promises, then as a woman, you may find yourself surrendering to sickness, boredom, negativism and defeat.

Rather than to acquiesce in life, resist with knowledge the tides of oppression, of religious discrimination, of pious inferiority, of doubt and of intimidation.

It is vital for *The Woman Believer* to understand that God created her to be a winner, to succeed, to be happy, to prosper, to be healthy, and to be an achiever in her own right.

The woman who does not discover herself in God's redemptive plan may surrender to a second-class status in life. This is what prejudicial religious dogmas and biased traditional doctrines seek to impose upon you.

The results of this social surrender can be tragic and traumatic for *The Woman Believer*. Loneliness and dissatisfaction may cloud your life. Lack of recognition and of personal achievement in your own name can discourage you. Your driving force of life can be stifled. Initiative and creativity can be smothered. Your vibrancy can diminish and you can mentally or psychologically die while you are still alive.

In this insidious process, despair can gradually overcome the woman who succumbs to social, economic and religious inequities. Buffeted by waves of fright and of irritation, you may experience times of anger and of resentment. Your language can reflect your inner emotions as your words become reactionary and ungracious.

You can be caught up in cycles of disillusionment and of negativism. You may feel trapped with no solution to your dilemma, as despair presses in upon you.

Woman's Arch-Enemy

Negative suggestions can come to your mind, that God is not concerned about women, that He may be punishing you for pride, for insubordination, or for rebellion against the *status quo.*

Opponents of *The Woman Believer* have never changed their tactics. The objective is always to cause believers to doubt God's promise, just as Satan suggested to Adam and Eve: *Has God said?*[1]

The enemy of *The Woman Believer* is relentless in his strategy to destroy faith in God. He knows that if we abandon faith in God, then we will have no faith in others. And ultimately — and most tragically, we will have no faith in ourselves as women.

Identity, Equality, Dignity

Must *The Woman Believer* struggle forever? No! It is time for her to realize peace and victory, self-realization and accomplishment, personal success and pride. Those things are a woman's birthright as a royal daughter in God's family?

The Woman Believer, literate and aware of her position in Christ, is no longer doomed to the subservient and submissive roles that have been historically prescribed by patriarchal theology.

The status of inferiority can no longer be imposed upon the believing woman, once she has discovered her birthright of identity, of equality, of dignity and of destiny in God's redemptive plan.

1.   Ge.3:1

Love does not see traditional and cultural barriers. Love sees the person of this Pokot tribeswoman with whom Daisy shares the message of Christ.

Chapter 37

FACTS OF A WOMAN'S BIRTHRIGHT

THE WORD *SALVATION* is the all-*inclusive* word that embraces all that Jesus provided for women through His death, burial and resurrection. According to Hebrew and Greek scholars, *salvation*[1] means: Rescue, safety, deliverance, forgiveness, protection, health, prosperity, preservation, freedom, liberty, peace, righteousness, victory. *Salvation* means, we are saved, recreated, healed, restored, made strong — and all of this applies to the whole person, spiritually, physically and materially. This is a woman's birthright.

Facts for *The Woman Believer*

Here are fourteen dynamic facts for *The Woman Believer*. They set forth some of a woman's birthright. Read them repeatedly and learn the scripture references I have included.

1. Jesus died so that you, a woman, might live.[2]

2. He took your sins and now gives you, a woman, His righteousness.[3]

3. He bore your emptiness and now gives you, a woman, His fullness.[4]

4. He carried your evil and now gives you, a

woman, His goodness.[5]

5.   He suffered your diseases and now gives you, a woman, His health.[6]

6.   Your defeats are wiped out and His success is now yours.[7]

7.   He took your failures and now gives you, a woman, His triumph.[8]

8.   As a woman, you are no longer in danger.[9]

9.   As a woman, you do not lose in battle.[10] The Lord is your victory.[11]

10.   As a woman, you are not weak nor inferior.[12] Christ is your strength and your security.[13]

11.   Sickness no longer dominates you, a woman, because the Lord is your physician.[14]

12.   As a woman, you are no longer in destitution and need.[15]   The Lord is your supply source.[16]

13.   As a woman, you no longer need to lack direction or to make wrong decisions.[17] The Lord is your shepherd and He guides you in every detail of your life.[18]

14.   As a woman, you are no longer alone and abandoned.[19] Jesus Christ is always with you.[20]

This is all part of your complete *salvation* which is a woman's birthright the same as it is the birthright of any man.

1.	He.5:9	5.	Col.2:13-15	13.	Ps.27:1
	1Pe.1:3-5		Ro.6:23		Ps.28:7
	He.2:3-4		Ep.3:17-19		Ps.118:14
	1Th.5:8-10	6.	Is.53:4		2 Co.2:14
	Ep.6:17		Mt.8:17	14.	Ex.15:26
	Ac.4:10-12	7.	1Jn.3:8		23:25
	Ro.10:10		Col.2:9-10		Ps.103:3
2.	Ro.5:6,17-18	8.	Ps.98:1-4	15.	Ps.23:1,5
	1Jn.3:16		1Co.15:57		Ps.31:19
	Ga.2:20		1Jn.5:4		Ps.84:11
3.	2Co.5:21	9.	Ps.91:1-11	16.	Ph.4:19
	1Pe.2:24		Ps.28:7-9		Ps.36:6-9
4.	Jn.1:16	10.	Ps.18:29		Ps.89:11
	1Co.1:30		Ps.41:10	17.	Ps.32:6-8
	Ep.2:12	11.	Ps.18:2		Ps.48:14
	Ep.2:18-20		Ph.4:13		Ps.73:23-24
	Ep.3:16-21	12.	Jl.3:10	18.	Ps.23:1
	1Pe.1:4		2Co.12:10		Pr.3:5-6
				19.	He.13:5
				20.	Mt.28:20

Daisy says, "I have discovered that women, worldwide, need to discover their identity, dignity, equality and destiny in God's plan." She shares Christ wherever she is (Top: Asia. Center: Africa. Bottom: S. America.)

Chapter 38

THIS IS YOUR HERITAGE

ANY WOMAN WHO embraces Christ as a living, present reality, can count on experiencing full victory in every phase of her life.[1]

When Jesus Christ suffered the punishment of a woman's sins and died in her place,[2] every count against her was wiped out.[3]

Three days after Christ's death, God raised Him from the dead according to the scriptures.[4] He rose in total victory over woman's adversary, Satan.[5]

He said, *Do not be afraid; I am He who lives, and was dead, and behold, I am alive forevermore ... and I have the keys of Hell and of Death.*[6]

As a woman, you can appreciate these scriptures. You will notice that I have personalized them for you.

New Lifestyle in Christ

You, being dead in your trespasses ... He has made alive together with Him, having forgiven you all trespasses. Having wiped out everything that was against you ... He took it out of the way, having nailed it to the cross. Having disarmed principalities and powers, He made a public spectacle of them, triumphing over them in it.[7]

Now you — a woman can say with Paul: *Like as Christ was raised up from the dead by the glory of the Father, even so I also walk in newness of life.*[8]

As a woman you can say: *In all these things, I am more than a conqueror through Him who loved me.*[9]

Now thanks be to God, who always causes me to triumph in Christ.[10]   *If God be for me, who can be against me.*[11] *For I am dead (to sin) and my life is hid with Christ in God.*[12]

For the Son of God was manifested, that He might destroy the works of the devil,[13] *and now I am of God ... and have overcome* (the devil) *because greater is He that is in me* (a woman), *than he that is in the world.*[14]

Jesus is the author of your *salvation* and it is complete. He died to provide all that any woman needs. His abundant life is now imparted to you.

As a woman, you have the victory. Christ is your captain. That is your birthright.

Nobody knows, more than Satan himself, what was accomplished for womankind through the death, burial and resurrection of Jesus Christ.

Satan struggles always to keep women from learning about it. If they do discover it, then he strives to make them doubt or question or deny it.

As long as Satan can make a woman doubt what Christ has done for her in His sacrifice, he can beat her in every battle.

Woman's Adversary Conquered

In the garden of Eden, Satan caused Adam and Eve to question God's word.[15]   They forfeited God's blessings and Satan enslaved them.[16]

Jesus said, Satan comes to *steal* and to *kill* and to *destroy*.[17]

The apostle Peter said, *Your enemy, the devil, walks about as a roaring lion, seeking whom he may devour.*[18]

But James said: *Resist the devil, and he will flee from you.*[19]

That explains why Paul said that a woman must *fight the good fight of faith*,[20] remembering that *the weapons of her warfare are not carnal, but mighty through God to the pulling down of strongholds.*[21]

The Woman Believer is to be strong in the Lord, and in the power of His might. She is to put on the whole armor of God, that she may be able to stand against the wiles of the devil. For she wrestles not against flesh and blood, but against principalities, against powers, against the rulers of the darkness of this world, against spiritual wickedness in high places.[22]

So for a woman to experience achievement in life, she must *take the whole armor of God, that she may be able to withstand in the evil day, and having done all, to stand, having her waist girded with truth, having on the breastplate of righteousness, and having her feet shod with the preparation of the gospel of peace; above all, taking the shield of faith, with which she shall quench all the fiery darts of the wicked one.*[23]

And take the helmet of salvation, and the sword of the Spirit, which is the word of God: praying always ... being watchful with all perseverance.[24]

When a woman accepts the risen Lord into her life as her Master and as the *author of her salvation*,[25] Christ dwells in that woman. That puts His whole armor upon her and He is her victory.

God says to you as a woman, right now: *Behold, I am the Lord, the God of all flesh; is there anything too hard for Me?*[26]

He promises *The Woman Believer: No weapon that is formed against you will prosper; and every tongue that shall rise against you in judgment you shall condemn. This is the heritage of the servants of the Lord.*[27]   That is a woman's birthright.

1.	Ro.8:37	10.	2Co.2:14	19.	Ja.4:7
2.	1Pe.2:24	11.	Ro.8:31	20.	1Ti.6:12
3.	Ro.8:1	12.	Col.3:3	21.	2Co.10:4
4.	1Co.15:4	13.	1Jn.3:8	22.	Ep.6:11-12
5.	Ep.1:20-22	14.	1Jn4:4	23.	Ep.6:13-16
6.	Re.1:17-18	15.	Ge.3:1-6	24.	Ep.6:17-18
7.	Col.2:13-15	16.	Ge.3:23-24	25.	He.5:9
8.	Ro.6:4	17.	Jn.10:10	26.	Je.32:27
9.	Ro.8:37	18.	1Pe.5:8	27.	Is.54:17

Chapter 39

YOUR INVINCIBLE PARTNER

WHEN GOD RAISED Jesus Christ from the dead to be our eternal Savior, He wanted *the eyes of your understanding* (as a woman) *to be enlightened, that you might know what ... are the riches of the glory of His inheritance in the saints, and what is the exceeding greatness of His power toward us* (women) *who believe, according to the working of His mighty power, which He worked in Christ when He raised Him from the dead and seated Him ... far above all principality and power and might and dominion, and every name that is named, not only in this age, but also in that which is to come.*[1]

And has quickened you (a woman) *together with Christ (by grace are you saved) and raised you up, and made you to sit in heavenly places in Christ Jesus.*[2]

Knowing this, *God has not given you* (a woman), *the spirit of fear; but of power, and of love, and of a sound mind.*[3]

As *The Woman Believer, you have the mind of Christ.*[4] *You have His wisdom and righteousness and sanctification and redemption.*[5] All that He is, He is in you as soon as you accept Him by faith.

For it pleased the Father that in Him (the Son) *should all fullness dwell.*[6] *And of His fullness have you* (a woman) *received.*[7] *For all things are yours.*[8]

That belongs to *The Woman Believer* the same as it does to any man who follows Christ.

According as His divine power has given to you, (a woman), all things that pertain to life ... whereby are given to you exceeding great and precious promises; that by these you might be partakers of the divine nature.[9]

So through the promises of God, you as a woman, have received Christ Himself, and His own nature is in you.

You are a royal daughter in God's family. You belong to royalty and Christ lives at your house.

What an inheritance!   What a birthright!

Triumph for Every Woman

The devil may roar, and threaten you as a woman, but John says that when you are *born of God* (in a new birth), *that wicked one touches you not.*[10]   Claim that as *The Woman Believer* that you are.

When Satan approaches you, he has the Lord to deal with. Christ lives at your house. You are no longer a loser in life. *Thanks be to God, who gives you the victory through our Lord Jesus Christ.*[11]

It was when Christ triumphed over principalities and powers through His death on the cross and through His resurrection, that He provided for every woman the victory over every foe.

He has delivered us (women) *from the power of darkness, and has translated us into the kingdom of His dear Son, in whom we have redemption through His blood.*[12]

The death of Christ on the cross signaled that all of your sins have been put away and that the devil can no longer condemn you. *The Woman Believer* is translated out of Satan's dominion and is restored to God's domain.

Satan knows all of this and therefore when you (a woman), *resist the devil, he will flee from you.*[13]

When God raised Jesus from the dead, He had the keys of hell and of death. His triumph over Satan was the triumph for every believing woman. His victory was your victory. He did it on your behalf. Now because He lives, you live also, energized by His own life.

Satan, your adversary, is conquered. Sin and evil, disease and suffering, poverty and failure have been defeated by Christ who came to *destroy the works of the devil*[14] for you, a woman.

He makes His abode at your house now. He has become your invincible partner.

Now is come salvation, and strength, and the kingdom of our God, and the power of His Christ: for the accuser of our brothers (and sisters) *is cast down, who accused them before God day and night. And they overcame him by the blood of the Lamb, and by the word of their testimony.*[15]

Now you are triumphant. Satan can no longer defeat *The Woman Believer* because He whose *name is called The Word of God*[16] dwells in her and she *has redemption through His blood.*[17]

1.	Ep.1:18:21	7.	Jn.1:16	13.	Ja.4:7
2.	Ep.2:5-6	8.	1Co.3:21	14.	1Jn.3:8
3.	2Ti.1:7	9.	2Pe.1:3-4	15.	Re.12:10-11
4.	1Co.2:16	10.	1Jn.5:18	16.	Re.19:13
5.	1Co.1:30	11.	1Co.15:57	17.	Col.1:14
6.	Col.1:19	12.	Col.1:13-14		

Chapter 40

CHRIST YOUR VICTORY

JESUS SAYS TO *The Woman Believer: All power (all authority) is given to me in heaven and earth ... and lo, I am with you alway, even to the end of the world.*[1]

So you as a woman, can say, *The life which I now live in the flesh, I live by the faith of the Son of God, who loved me, and gave Himself for me.*[2]

You can say, *All things are mine ... and I am Christ's, and Christ is God's.*[3]

Christ came to give you, *The Woman Believer* abundant life.[4] He fought your battles and won your victory. He dealt with your enemy and you should never think of Satan, except as a defeated foe.[5] His power or jurisdiction over you is finished. You are free.

When the devil comes to you as a woman believer, he must deal with Christ who conquered him.

When Satan touches you, he touches God's property.

When problems arise, think of Christ as your answer.

If sickness assails you, remember that the life of Jesus is in you,[6] physically[7] as well as spiritually.[8]

If condemnation or guilt nags you about past sins, remember that they are washed away and that God sees you only in the light of Christ's righteousness.[9]

When confusion and despair overwhelm you, remember that Christ is your peace.[10]

If economic circumstances get tough and you wonder how you can make ends meet, think about the Creator, your Father, who is the source of all riches. He lives at your house. His wealth is yours now.[11]

When you feel lonely or afraid, hear Christ say, *Lo, I am with you.*[12]

When problems and battles confront you, do not forget that the Lord is your victory; that Satan must now deal with Jesus Christ whenever he attacks or tempts you.[13]

Jesus is yours. You are His. Together, you are an unbeatable team. Your partner in life is invincible. That is every woman's birthright.

Prayer for Victory

This is the victory that overcomes the world, even our faith.[14]

Pray this prayer sincerely and with faith:

DEAR LORD JESUS:

Before I understood why You died on the cross for me, I faced a life of problems. Fears and threats tormented me. There was little peace in my soul. Sickness was a thief and a destroyer that threatened to cut me down.

I faced perplexities and distress. I was confused. Solutions evaded me.

Now I know that my enemy is Satan who robbed Adam and Eve of their paradise. I was his slave too because of my life of sin.

But now *I know the truth, and the truth has set me free.*[15] Now I know that You went to the cross on my behalf. You died for me. You met Satan face to face on my behalf, and accepted all of the punishment that I deserved. You paid my account in full. You died under the load of my sins.

Through your death for me, You stripped Satan of all authority over my life.[16] You arose from the dead and lifted me out of his domain.[17] I was translated into Your kingdom and was made a member of Your family.[18]

I have heard this good news and I believe it.[19] Today You have become the author of my *salvation.*[20]

Your word says: *If anyone is in Christ Jesus, he or she is a new creature: old things are passed away; behold, all things are become new.*[21]

That has happened to me. You have made me a new creature. My new life is Your life.

Instead of sins and guilt and fear, I have salvation and righteousness and peace.[22]

Instead of confusion and defeat, I have direction and success.[23]

Instead of disease and sickness, I have health and strength.[24]

Instead of weakness and inability, *I can do all things through Christ.*[25]

Instead of poverty and lack, I am rich with Christ.[26] God, the Creator of all wealth, is my Father who wills for me His success, blessing and prosperity.

Instead of loneliness and fear, You are now living at my house and blessing my life.

Instead of struggles and lost battles, now I am a winner because You are the author of my salvation and I cannot lose.

Oh, thank You, Lord. Now my life has meaning and purpose.

If God be for me (and with me and in me) *who can be against me?*[27]

The Lord is the strength of my life; of whom shall I be afraid?[28]

In all these things, I am more than conqueror through You, Lord, who loved me. For I am persuaded that neither death, nor life, nor angels, nor principalities, nor powers, nor things present, nor things to come, nor height, nor depth, nor any other creature, shall be able to separate me from the love of God, which is in You, dear Jesus, MY LORD.[29]

* * *

Now you have learned vital facts about your divine heritage as *The Woman Believer*. Act on these truths. Put them to the test. Practice applying them in your life and in your relations with others.

God has invested as much in you as a woman, as He has in any man. He believes in you. He trusts you. He lives through you to bless others. You have discovered the benefits of a woman's birthright. Now act on those benefits.

1.	Mt.28:18,20	11.	Ga.4:7	19.	Ro.1:16
2.	Ga.2:20		Ro.8:16-17	20.	He.2:10
3.	1Co.3:21-23	12.	Mt.28:20	21.	2Co.5:17
4.	Jn.10:10		He.13:5	22.	Ep.1:7-13
5.	1Jn.3:8	13.	Is.59:19		Ph.3:9
	Col.2:12-15		Ro.8:31,37		Ro.5:1
6.	2Co.4:10-11		1Jn.5:18	23.	Pr.3:5-6
7.	Ro.8:11	14.	1Jn.5:4		Jos.1:8
8.	Jn.10:10	15.	Jn.8:32	24.	Ps.27:1
9.	Ro.3:24-25	16.	Re.1:18		2Co.4:11
	Re.1:5	17.	Col.1:13	25.	Ph.4:13
	1Co.6:11	18.	Ep.2:19	26.	2Co.8:9
10.	Ep.2:14		3:14-15	27.	Ro.8:31
	Col.1:19-21		1Pe.2:9	28.	Ps.27:1
				29.	Ro.8:37-39

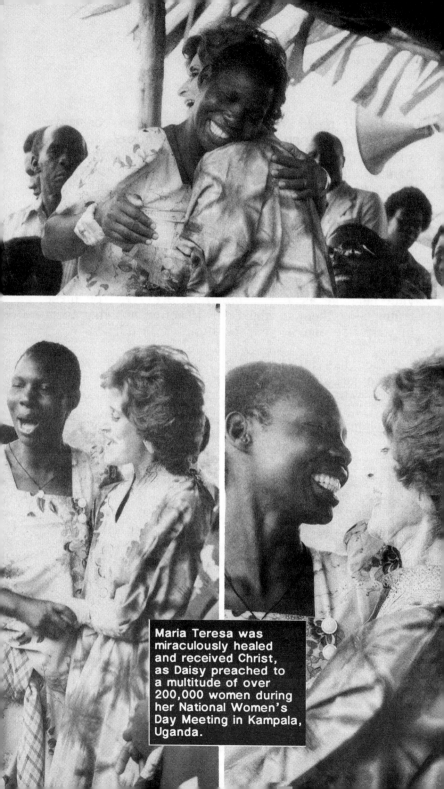

Maria Teresa was miraculously healed and received Christ, as Daisy preached to a multitude of over 200,000 women during her National Women's Day Meeting in Kampala, Uganda.

PART IX

THE
LOVE
IDEA
FOR
WOMEN

CAN WHAT THE Bible calls salvation be a practical experience for women, in the same full sense that it is represented for men, without being tarnished by sex discrimination?

Is God as interested in women as His friends and co-workers as He is in men?

Must enlightened and redeemed women in this century continue to acquiesce before demeaning church dogmas and the traditions handed down from medieval epochs?

Educated women no longer sustain these antiquated indignities. *The Woman Believer* today has made new choices to cultivate the self-value and the self-esteem necessary for her to take her place in God's redemptive plan, and to fulfill her rightful role in lifting her world to Christ.

God's love idea embraces every woman as it does every man, drawing them and restoring them to His side as His partners and friends in giving life and love to people.

Chapter 41

HOW GOD VALUES WOMEN

WOMEN ARE MADE for life, not for death; for health, not for disease; for success, not for failure.

God wants no woman — or man — to live without hope, or to be alone without friends, or to be unhappy. He wants no one to live in shame, or fear, or disgrace.

He paid a big price for you as a woman, which proves your divine worth to Him. That is God's love idea for women.

Love is the greatest idea ever to come from God to human beings. There is *faith and hope and love, but the greatest of these is love.*[1]

The Bible says: *God is love.*[2] You as a woman, are created by God. You are the creation of love.

God loves you, a woman, so much that He paid the same price to have you near Him as He paid to have any man near Him. He paid the price of His Son. That underscored how much God values you.

The Healing Power of Love

One day a leper came to Jesus. The essence of the story is: The disciples said, *Send him away. He is unclean.* But Jesus said: *No, let him* come. *He has faith.*[3]

The purpose of Christ's coming was to help, to save and to bless people. Love caused our Lord to reach out His hand and to touch that leper, and his flesh was instantly healed.

One day some men brought a woman to Jesus whom they accused of adultery. The essence of that story is similar to that of the leper: Self-righteous men said, *Let's stone her to death. She is an unclean woman.*[4]

But Jesus said: *Wait a minute. God did not send His Son into the world to condemn the world, but to save the world.*[5] You see, God's love idea is that He values each human person.

He forgave that woman's sins, made her pure and clean again and restored her self-dignity and her self-esteem as a lady.

It is impossible for Him to accuse or judge or condemn you. His value of you as a woman, is so great that He seeks to lift and to bless you, to help you to become all that your heavenly Father created you to be. That is God's love idea for women.

The Prostitute Believed

In one of our crusades, a young woman who had practiced prostitution since she was a teenager, attended and heard us teaching about God's love for women and for men.

She came because a large cancerous tumor had developed in her womb. Physically, she was a terminal case; she was socially rejected; and she was not even thirty years old.

She wept as she learned that Jesus Christ had come to this world on her behalf and had already assumed the guilt, condemnation and judgment of all of her sins. She came to understand that Jesus had already suffered the penalty that she herself deserved; that He had done it in order to redeem her and to restore her to God as though she had never committed a wrong.

God Already Did His Part

She learned that the cross of Jesus proved several things:

1) That she was valued by God.

2) That she was loved by God.

3) That her sins had already been punished.

4) That God cared for her even before she knew about Him.

5) That God had already redeemed her and that all she had to do was to hear about His love, to believe it and to accept it.

That woman trusted in what Jesus accomplished on her behalf. She accepted Him and His life in her, and she was saved.

Instantly, as she was thanking God for His love, the big tumor disappeared. It was a miracle. She was totally healed. She was at peace with

God who had come home to live in her. And she
had come home to Him.

You see, God's love idea for women is the
happy news that He wants to restore them because
He loves them. He never destroys anyone — not
their health, not their happiness, not their reputa-
tion, certainly not their self-esteem.

God wants to do good things for you today.
His love is in action now. He wants to do for you
a woman, whatever you need or desire, if you will
only believe in His love idea for you.

1.   1Co.13:13   4.   Jn.8:3-11
2.   1Jn.4:8   5.   Jn.3:17
3.   Mk.1:40-42

Chapter 42

TRANSFORMING POWER

AS JESUS CLIMBED out of a boat one day, a wild man came running from among the tombs. Night and day this poor creature screamed and cut himself with stones. He was tormented by demons.

Jesus spoke to the evil spirits and they came out of the man and he was healed.[1]

That is what Christ came for. He never wants a human person to live in shame or fear or disgrace. He values people — every woman, the same as every man and every child — and He will do whatever you need in order to develop your finest potential.

Love for the Maniac

A young man was brought to one of our crusades. He was a former medical student. For some reason his mind had snapped, and he had become insane.

The man's classmates had strapped his hands and feet with crude iron bands, then they had chained him so that he could not escape because he was a menace even to himself.

They had taken the insane man back to his village, where his family had kept him bound in chains and locked in a hut with a door made of crossed poles, wired together, to allow ventilation.

Food was tossed to him like one would feed a dangerous animal. He would lunge at people as they passed his hut, trying to bite them. Someone had kicked him in the mouth and had knocked his front teeth out.

Four men brought him to the crusade. They had chained and gagged him to prevent his biting someone.

As we shared the gospel of God's love idea, the demon spirits went out of the insane man and he became perfectly normal.

They removed the gag from his mouth and the chained bands which had caused thick callouses on his wrists and ankles.

He resumed his medical studies at the university and is a living witness of God's love idea.

You Were Created for Love

Why does God love you so much? Why did Jesus give His life for you? Why did He die in your place? Why has God's love idea been sent to you through this book?

Because He values you just as you are.

Proof that God has chosen to reach out to you as a woman, is evident: This book is in your hands. Whatever you need or desire from God has already begun.

1.   Mk.5:2-8,15

Chapter 43

THE LOVE IDEA FOR FRANCE

A FRENCH TEACHER spending her vacation in America, visited *International Gospel Center* and the world missions offices of our Tulsa, Oklahoma church headquarters.

Since she spoke practically no English, our French translator hosted the lady.

The impact of our international church ministries provoked many questions about our *programme d'évangélisation, religion et doctrine.*

Our translator took advantage of her questions to witness about Christ. She explained the simplicity of what we teach. It is Jesus, not a religion, but a person — the Son of God who assumed the guilt of our sins and suffered the judgment we deserved in order to free us from all guilt and to restore us to God as though we had never sinned.

To the French lady, this seemed too simplistic to be valid. Her questions: "Why evangelize people of other lands such as Hindus, Buddhists, Moslems? They are content in their religions. Why should we believe that ours is better?

"How can we be sure that God exists? That Jesus is His Son, or that He was born of a virgin? Why was His death any different than that of any other person? Or His blood more divine than that of anyone else? Why are we sure that He was raised from the dead? Why do we believe that the Bible is true?"

Should We Ask Questions?

Then, of course, to reassure her hostess that she was not a pagan: "You know, I have my religion. After all, we aren't savages! But anyone who thinks or reads or has average intelligence, must ask questions. You see, I'm a divorcée with two children to raise. I wonder about them without a father, to face an uncertain future. As a divorcée, am I not automatically out of the church? Why not just end it, once and for all?

"If I simply follow your counsel and welcome Jesus into my heart and trust Him, what are the prayers I should recite? What are the sins I should abstain from? To just receive Jesus and to believe that He comes and lives in me, is that all? Should I not first try to improve myself?

"In my predicament are you saying I can pray and know God and relate to Him as my friend? As my Father? And He will help me? Why has no one told me this before? I've been confused for many years.

"Every time anyone talks to me about religion, I get the impression that they want to enlist me in something, in their church or their denomination. But you've talked to me without clichés or religious bigotry. I have the feeling that there is hope for me, that Jesus is the way, that the gospel is put into true perspective, and that my own life now has purpose."

She left with a newly discovered life-pattern in Jesus Christ. The New Testament would be her guide. Some of our books given to her by our translator, fortified the decision she had made to follow Jesus.

She had discovered that God loved and valued her as a woman, as much as He loved and valued any other person on earth. She had learned about God's love idea for women.

Good, Big, Loving, Powerful

Women all over the world are searching for purpose in their lives, for the reality of God, for evidence that the Bible is true — and if so, how to make a practical application of it in their individual lives.

Why is the cross of Christ so important and what does it mean to a woman today? Why the constant guilt of sin and wrong doing? What is the way for a woman to really find peace with God?

If God is good and if He created women in His own image, why are the minds of so many women confused? Why are they the victims of so much discrimination, fear, bigotry, loneliness and guilt?

If God is a woman's creator, why do so many of them continue to live in subservience and in inferiority? Why are so many of their prayers unanswered? Why are so many women religious while so few of them experience satisfying reality? Why do women have so much knowledge and yet have so few answers to the religious and cultural dilemmas in which they are so often trapped?

What causes loneliness, depression and suicide among so many women?

Why is there so much family turmoil, divorce, violence, brutality?

Chapter 44

LIFE AND LOVE FOR WOMEN

CAN WHAT THE Bible calls salvation be a practical experience for women, in the same full sense that it is represented for men, without sexual bias or discrimination?

Is God interested in women as His friends and co-workers?

Does He want women to have health, happiness, success and prosperity in this life?

Is it His plan for women to set goals and to achieve them? To represent Him to people? To be His ambassadors? To receive His Holy Spirit and to be His witnesses in all the world?

Does God trust women?

Must a woman live in subjugated mediocrity in order to have true humility and to be close to God?

Can sickness and pain be the will of our heavenly Father for women — or for anyone — when an earthly mother would never desire that her own children be diseased?

The business world believes in solving its problems. But if a woman poses questions about her position in Christ or about her circumscribed ministry in the church, she can be regarded as rebellious or insubordinate.

The average Christian woman is usually well enough "indoctrinated" that she tends to ignore logical questions which concern her dignity and her equality in God's redemptive plan and in Christian ministry.

She often defends her prescribed limits in the church, embracing illogical and discriminating doctrines and dogmas which relegate her to inferiority and to subservience — a status which contradicts the redemptive work of Christ.

Must enlightened and redeemed women in this century continue to acquiesce before demeaning church traditions, handed down from medieval epochs, which restrict their Christian ministry in today's world?

It is tragic that, due to these illogical and outdated restraints imposed by church pontificates, millions of intelligent women have abandoned the idea of faith in God. They have relegated Him and the Bible to little more than a concept and a book of outdated delusions. They have reached these unfortunate conclusions because of hard-nosed and chauvinistic clergymen who insist on restraining women's Christian ministries to the levels of ancient cultures for reasons which have no relevance to progressive societies today.

Educated, modern women no longer sustain these antiquated double standards. *The Woman Believer* today has learned to make redemption-based choices in order to cultivate the self-value and the self-esteem necessary for her to take her place in God's plan, and to fulfill her rightful role in lifting her world to Christ.

I am happy to tell you that God is as good and as big and as loving and as powerful as the Bible says He is. *For God is good, and He loves goodness.*[1] *There is nothing but goodness in Him.*[2] *There is nothing too hard for Him.*[3]

1.   Ps.11:7 LB
2.   Ps.92:15 LB
3.   Je.32:17

Daisy believes that the greatest achievement in life is to bring the gospel of Jesus to people, as she does here to a multitude in E. Africa.
Inset: She rejoices with a Hindu lady who was a deaf-mute since birth and who has been healed as Daisy ministered to the field of people.

Chapter 45

LOVE FOR OUR WORLD

FOR OVER FOUR DECADES, my husband and I have shared the message of the love of God with multitudes of from 20,000 to 250,000 people nightly. We have proven, thousands of times, that God is what He says He is; that He will do what He says He will do; that the Bible is real and that what it says is as true for women as it is for men.

We have witnessed abundant proof that God is real, that Jesus Christ is alive, and that His miracle-working power is unchanged today.

Every time we see cancers healed, paralytics walk, blind and deaf people restored; every time we see unhappy lives transformed, or defeated, poverty-level families discover God's abundant living and prosperity, we see Him at work.

We see the miracle of His seeds reproducing His wholeness in the lives of those who believe in Him. We see the marvelous fruits of God's love idea at work in human persons.

Re-Living the Gospels

When T.L. and I went to India as missionaries, we were very young. We wanted to share God's love with those who had not heard the good news of Christ. We had not yet learned the secrets of simple faith in God's promises and of how to act upon His word. Consequently, there were no miracles to give proof of what we taught.

But as a result of this experience, our own lives were transformed. The Lord Jesus Christ showed Himself to each of us, though at different times and in distinct appearances. These events made us know that He is more than a religion — that He is alive. The Bible became a living book for us.

We discovered the principles of God's love idea and how His miracles are all contained in the seeds of the promises which He has given us to plant in human lives. We have been re-living the gospels of Christ during most of our lives as we have ministered to millions, face to face, around the world.

Every day our mail contains exciting testimonies of miracles and of changed lives that come to us from nations abroad.

So many women write to me about their problems and hurts, about their struggles and sicknesses, about their needs and difficulties.

Let me share some of God's love idea with you. Let me show you how you as a woman, can become more than you ever dreamed of becoming, how you can be healed and blessed, how you can succeed and prosper, how you can have God as your partner in life, and how you can become *The Woman Believer*.

When you hear God's promises and believe them, you will be planting his miracle seeds in your life. They will produce what they say.

You are going to find yourself right in the middle of God's abundant living. You will look up one of these days, and discover a harvest of good things growing up all around you.

No Longer Guilty

A troubled man attended one of our mass crusades in Latin America. From his youth, he had hated protestant Christians. He and his friends would ambush them in the countryside, rob them of their belongings and often beat them. He told us that he had even helped to kill some of them.

Jesus Christ had become real to his wife soon after they were married. For nineteen years she had prayed that her husband would have a personal encounter with the Lord.

The man attended our crusade and, for the first time in his life, realized that God had created human persons to walk and talk with Him in the garden of His presence; that human persons are made in God's own image and since God is love, that it is His plan for each individual believer to share His love; that hatred, evil and murder are from Satan who caused humanity to sin against God from the beginning.

That dear man had never heard the gospel before. As he listened, the death of Christ suddenly became a living reality to him.

You Are Already Forgiven

Later, the man told us, "As I began to think about the brutal acts I had committed against

innocent people, I realized that I had helped nail
Jesus to that cross.   I visualized Him hanging
there, enduring the punishment of my sins so that I
would not be held guilty before God.

"As you taught, you made me realize that I was
the one who should have been crucified.

"I wanted to cry out, 'Why you, Lord?   Why
are You being crucified?   I was the one they should
have crucified!'"

That dear man, with his devoted wife standing
beside him, fell to his knees and accepted Christ's
forgiveness.   He realized that God held none of his
sins against him.   He had embraced God's love
idea.

Chapter 46

LOVE'S MIRACLE LIFE

EVERY WOMAN NEEDS to realize that the word "forgiven" means "to grant relief from payment of a debt or obligation." Jesus Christ paid the penalty of every woman's sins forever.

If you as a woman, believe on Christ, then I can assure you that there is absolutely no sin which can be held against you. You shall never have to face God's judgment for your sins if you embrace the fact that Jesus did that in your name, when He suffered the judgment of your sins, in your place, on the cross.

Jesus said, *I say emphatically that anyone who believes in God who sent Me has eternal life, and will never be damned* (or condemned or judged) *for his or her sins, but has already passed out of death into life.*[1]

There is now no condemnation to those who are in Christ Jesus,[2] *for who shall accuse those whom God has chosen? God Himself declares them not guilty! Can anyone, then, condemn them? ... Jesus Christ is the one who died* (for them) ... *who then can separate us from the love of Christ?*[3]

As far as the east is from the west, so far has He removed our transgressions from us.[4]

God's redemption provides the way for you as a woman, to be restored to God as though no sin had ever been committed in your life.

I will outline for you the seven basic steps to take, in order to personally accept God's love idea for women and to become *The Woman Believer*.

FIRST: Believe You Are Valuable As God's Creation

God created humankind in His own image[5] *... in the likeness of God.*[6]

SECOND: Know That Distrusting God's Word Is the Original and Basic Problem

Eve took of the fruit and ate it, and gave some to her husband with her; and he ate it.[7]

That was the original sin — distrusting God's word which had warned them that they would die.

THIRD: Understand That Disavowing God's Integrity Results in Death

God said, in the day that you (disavow my instructions and) *eat the fruit I forbade, you will surely die.*[8]

The wages of sin (disavowing the integrity of God's word) *is death.*[9]

FOURTH: Believe That God Values You Too Much to Let You Die

God so loved the world that He gave His only begotten Son, that whoever believes in Him will not perish, but have everlasting life.[10]

FIFTH: Know Why Jesus Came and Died As Your Substitute

Jesus Christ bore your sins in His own body, that you, having died to sins, might live for righteousness.[11]

SIXTH: Understand the Reason for Christ's Death, Burial and Resurrection

A.   When Jesus Christ died, your old life of sin died with Him.

You have been crucified with Christ.[12]

B.   When Jesus Christ was buried, your old life of sin was put away forever.

You are buried with Jesus Christ into death.[13]

C.   When Jesus Christ was raised from the dead, you were raised up with Him.

Like as Christ was raised up from the dead by the glory of the Father, even so you also should walk in newness of life.[14]

You are risen with Christ. Christ is your life.[15]

SEVENTH: Believe the Gospel and Receive Jesus Christ in Person Now

Believe on the Lord Jesus Christ and you will be saved.[16]

As many as receive Jesus Christ, He gives to them power to become the children of God.[17]

* * *

Now say these seven things to God:

1.   I believe I am valuable as Your own creation.

2.   Now I understand that to doubt Your word is the basic sin.

3.   I know that the wages of sin is deterioration and eternal death.

4.   I thank You for valuing me too much to let me die in my sins.

5.   I believe Jesus Came died in my place, suffered the penalty of my sins, and redeemed me forever.

6.   I realize three great facts:
(a)   When Jesus died for my sins, my old life died.
(b)   When Jesus was buried, my old life was buried.
(c)   When Jesus was raised in new life, His new life was offered to me.

7.   I now believe the gospel of Jesus Christ and I accept Him as my personal Savior and Lord, to live IN ME. From this moment, I am saved and *I am* restored to God.

1.	Jn.5:24 LB	7. Ge.3:6	13. Ro.6:4
2.	Ro.8:1	8. Ge.2:17	14. Ro.6:4
3.	Ro.8:33-35 TEV	9. Ro.6:23	15. Col.3:1,3
4.	Ps.103:12	10. Jn.3:16	16. Ac.16:31
5.	Ge.1:27	11. 1Pe.2:24	17. Jn.1:12
6.	Ge.5:1-2	12. Ga.2:20	

Fill in and sign this confession right now, and keep it as a record of your decision.

TODAY, on this ____ day of _____, 19___, I have read *The Woman Believer*. I believe on Jesus Christ, that He died in my name to redeem me from my sins. I accept Jesus as my Lord and Savior and I will serve Him all of my life.

Signed_____

After inviting people to believe on the Lord Jesus and to accept Him, Daisy rejoices with a business woman (top) and a Moslem man who have been converted to Christ.

Daisy gives of herself, of her time, of her abilities and of her talents to help make her world a better place.

Daisy teaches thousands of African women during her National Women's Ministry Seminar in Kenya's Nyanza province.

Daisy Osborn conducts a National Women's mass meeting at Kampala, with over 200,000 women in attendance—besides men and children.

Daisy conducts a National Women's Conference at Accra, Ghana.

Daisy preaches and ministers at African Women's Conference — Nigeria.

At Osborn Soulwinners' Institute — Kenya.

At Mission Convention — Norway.

At National Women's Conference — USA.

Daisy Osborn, a dynamic preacher of hope and courage, inspires both women and men to discover their destiny as winners on God's team. Throngs come to hear her daily at the Municipal Stadium Grounds, Mombasa, Kenya.

T.L. AND DAISY OSBORN CRUSADES

AFRICA

S. AMERICA

INDONESIA

CARIBBEAN

PHILIPPINES